Let the Bees Buzz

FINDING REDEMPTION IN THE AFTERMATH OF SCHOOL BULLYING

TAMI MCCANDLISH

Book Design & Production:
Columbus Publishing Lab
www.ColumbusPublishingLab.com

LCCN: 2023900389

Paperback ISBN: 978-1-63337-710-3
E-Book ISBN: 978-1-63337-711-0

Printed in the United States of America
1 3 5 7 9 10 8 6 4 2

To Charlie, Mom, Dad, Mattie,
Tony, Rill, and Dell.

*"They swarmed around me like bees,
but they were consumed as quickly as burning thorns."
Psalm 118:12*

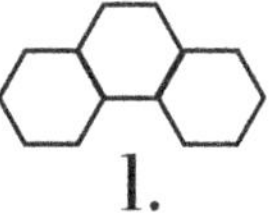

1. WHEN A SWARM SOUNDS

I THOUGHT I'D END my senior year of high school laughing like my classmates. While they planned for Skip Day, shopped for prom, and rehearsed the glorious moment we had long awaited, I stared at a shotgun cabinet. A girl can only take so much.

They were my playpen buddies, my sleepover secrets, my hugs in the hallways, and my praise in the stands. Some of us would venture to college, some would cross the county line, and a handful would move out of state, but I thought all of us would return. Like our parents, we'd shake hands across the pump at the Quick Stop, gather before kickoff, and catch up in the aisles of the grocery store. I thought I'd always have home because I'd always have them. Until one reaction changed everything, and they gossiped me nearly to the grave.

Twenty years later, as much as I'd like to forget, social media keeps memories alive. A teammate tags me in an old photograph of the homecoming parade. I flush and find myself back in the locker room, where I see her silent amidst chaos. I thought if I accepted her friend request, she might mention what we went through. I'm open to reconciliation. I still want it more than I'd like to admit. But she's remained quiet on social media these last ten years—until now, leaving me puzzled as to whether this post is sadistic or simply her way of trying to start a conversation with me. Of all our moments, why did she share this? I brace myself for criticism, but I'm more invisible now than the day I left school. She and our classmates reel off nostalgia, agreeing that the past feels like yesterday, yet so long ago. While they wish to return, I'm reminded of what I don't want to remember. Why are the words and actions that wounded me so deeply so easily forgettable to them?

As the comments slow, I tell myself to close the window, but my cursor pops up a preview of two sweethearts who built a life together. Miniature versions of them sport our alma mater's colors, and I wonder if they see us in their kids. Do they teach their children to play school like they played, or are their sons and daughters coming home in tears?

One peek leads to another. I see an athlete's trophy transformed into a sparkling SUV. Cheerleaders recently reunited over breakfast. A girl I rode the bus with is a stay-at-home mom. She earned a vacation for selling candles. Do they realize they've achieved the kinds of things they bullied me for?

"Good for you," I mutter, rolling my eyes. I return to the photograph of the homecoming parade, remove the tag, and unfollow the post. I had distanced myself from them long enough that I thought I had mastered forgiveness. But when they jump back into my life through the screen, I realize it's a lot easier to love my enemies when I don't see them. My sarcasm reminds me that forgiveness is a choice, and sometimes I have to disregard my emotions when they don't align with my beliefs.

I no longer wish ill on those who bullied me. I just want to see something that tells me they've learned. Beyond profile pictures and job titles, I'm curious about who they became, what influenced their hearts and minds, and how it affects the world around them. I want to know that what we went through meant something to them like it meant something to me, to know that we're all better for the experience.

Of the classmates I reconnected with, most never mention what happened. Some say they had no idea. Most likely I'm an afterthought to them, if they think of me at all. But a day doesn't pass without me thinking about what happened and how it shaped my life.

As a teenager, I thought that everyone was against me, that no one understood. I was a good girl gone bad, my character forever tainted, unworthy of forgiveness and incapable of overcoming the judgment of my peers.

Throughout college and into adulthood, I believed I was a social misfit. I saw the evidence through failed friendships, business clients who left without explanation, unextended party invitations, messages seen but never answered, and deletions on social media. Each occurrence traced a path to every relationship that had teased my trust and ended without warning, back to the hallways where I first learned to expect the worst.

One familiar pang could prompt a whole swarm of lies: *What's wrong with me* led to *no one notices me. No one notices me* meant *no one likes me. No one likes me* became *I'm repulsive. I can't keep friends. I'm not worth anyone's time.* I created problems that didn't exist. Over the years I've learned how to stop this barrage, but that doesn't mean I never hear the lies. Sometimes they still sneak up on me and threaten to pull me back into the shame that tells me that who I am turns others away. Now I recognize that those lies are nothing more than an entry for the enemy, and just because I hear them doesn't mean I need to entertain them. I rely on one voice to stop the warfare in my mind: the voice of the King of the Outcasts, who transformed rejection into honor and freed me from the shame of my youth.

Bullying was meant to harm me, but God worked it for my good. What I once thought was the worst thing to happen to me led me to my most cherished gift. Never again will I lose myself in the opinions of others. Never again will the heartbreak of lost friendship and community devalue my identity. Who I am isn't up for vote. In Jesus, I'm unrivaled royalty. For His glory, I forgive what's hard to forget, striving to love again as innocently as I loved then.

I write this story to the best of my recollection. Where possible, I confirmed my experiences with photographs, notes in yearbooks and shoeboxes, transcripts, emails, and a public incident report. Even so, my perspective is only one perspective and is as subjective as anyone's. To protect my characters' identities, I've changed names and certain revealing details. It's not my intention to prove who was right or wrong. I don't share my story to scold my characters or seek revenge. I share my story because I believe it reaches beyond the rivalry of two girls, our families, our friends, beyond our school district and hometown, and beyond adolescence.

This book is for the girl who struggles with competition and conflict with other girls. It's for the girl whose character and achievements incite name-calling, gossip, schemes, and silent treatments. It's for the girl who does her best to act nicely but is tired of hearing, "Ignore them." For the girl who stands up when systems fail only to receive a black mark on her permanent record. For the girl who loses her place amongst the people she loves most. The girl who doubts she can take one more day of school or life. If you are her, may the words that saved me save you too. Your life is not your own. You are not who they say you are. You are who God says you are. You're known, loved, and worth far more than a world of opinions. Bullying can't break you when you embrace your value in the One who made you.

This book is also for those who come from places like me, where people know you mostly by what they knew of you in high school. It's for those who can't remember what you had for lunch yesterday but can vividly recall the moments in school that crushed your spirit. It's for those who never received apologies. For those like the forty-year-old who told me, "I'll never forgive them for what they did to me." For those who combat loneliness and struggle to connect with others as a result of betrayal. And for those who've looked inward only to discover you need something bigger than yourself to overcome what was done to you.

The day we left school was the day the world told us to get over it. Adults expected us to outgrow the damage, and in many ways we did. We became adults who earned degrees, worked stable jobs, built businesses and families, and bought houses, cars, and vacations. It's the mature way of coping and the best form of revenge, according to the world. But isn't it also mature to admit what bothers and influences us and grow from our challenges? We don't have to bury the past under a pile of denial. Admitting that memories still sting doesn't make us immature. There's something we can do about all the hurt heaped on us long ago, the hurt we still secretly carry around in one way or another.

When the sins of seventeen filter into adulthood and the scars of adolescence reopen, I hope my story is a reminder that you aren't the names they called you or the things they did to you. Our stories may mirror one another, or maybe they're vastly different. Mine focuses on relational aggression, but there are certainly other forms of bullying, as well as others who endured far worse than I did. No matter the details, our stories don't diminish one another. There's purpose in what we each went through if we choose to seek it. Whether your experience occurred yesterday or twenty years ago, you can reflect on what happened while embracing freedom from what happened. There is healing when we open ourselves to the transformational power of Jesus, who, being bullied to the most severe extent, showed us how to forgive our enemies, renew our minds, love again, and move forward in friendship.

2. BLUE-COLLAR BINGO KID

MOST PEOPLE DON'T THINK of Ohio as much more than cornfields and boring, but I like to think of my home, located just outside the Hocking Valley region, as one of its best parts. Every time I drive back to that map dot at the edge of the Midwest, where farmland rolls into the foothills of Appalachia, my appreciation for it grows.

I grew up outside of a village built by an oil boom. In the early 1900s, people flooded the area hoping to gain wealth, and gain they did. Determined men used an early form of fracking—dropping nitroglycerin down wells to blast into the sand—to cause a geyser-like eruption of black gold. This was called "shooting" a well. Once they mastered the process, so many oil derricks lined Main Street that it was said one could climb from derrick to derrick without touching the ground. Oil money paved the way for brick streets and grand Victorian homes. The area thrived, and other industries, like lumber, glassware, and sand mining, prospered. Archives reveal my family's name associated with a restaurant, a car dealership, a trucking company, the bank, and a burial vault company, the latter of which was owned by my great-grandfather.

The oil boom lasted until the Great Depression, and the town never saw growth like that again. Many people returned to farming, raising livestock and crops on the rich alluvial soil of our valley. Generations later, agriculture remains at the heart of industry, and one of the only obvious reminders of the town's oil heyday is a reconstructed derrick that stands in the community park.

Every few years I drive back to that town of 1,200, ushered in by the remnants of the fiberglass factory, the empty glassware building, and rows of fifteen-foot steel storage tanks manufactured by a company that still supplies equipment for the gas and oil industry.

In a world of rapid changes, I'm comforted by what remains the same there. As I weave my way through the tree-lined streets, I pass my elementary school playground, the Tasty Freeze where Dad took me after biddy ball wins, and the church where I learned to sing "Up From the Grave He Arose." I recall who lived where and see that some people never left. One of my old bus drivers waves when I drive by, not because it's me but because he waves at everyone. It still makes me feel ten years old and important. I pass the house of my best friend from high school. Her mom is weeding the flower bed. I could stop to find out what happened to her daughter, but I keep driving. Across tidy yards, neighbors talk. Their daughters draw on the sidewalk with chalk. They remind me of me and my friends when we looked at each other more than screens. I crack my window to listen, and I feel at peace. These familiar sights and sounds make the world feel safer. When I was eighteen, I couldn't wait to leave that place, but now I'm reminded of how much I love it.

• • •

I'm from where my dad's from. We ran around that same town, attended the same school, and had some of the same teachers. Many of my classmates' parents were his classmates. We were both outgoing and known for our accomplishments. He was a successful trumpet player in the marching band, and I was a member of our school's all-time winningest basketball team. Dad was also known for his temper. He raised a ruckus in the parking lot and fought jocks who tried to give him a swirly. Some of those jocks, or their friends or relatives, became my teachers. I didn't know about his history with those teachers when I was in school, but I always wondered why they raised their eyebrows when I said hello, like they were waiting for me to mess up so they could send me to the principal's office. Did they see me and remember how a group of jocks failed to give one marching band member a dunk in the commode? Maybe it was my imagination. Or maybe they saw my dad's temperament in me before I noticed it in myself.

There has always been something in me that makes me clench my fists when I feel mistreated. When I was five, a carny at the county fair told me I could win a three-foot-tall stuffed Spuds MacKenzie doll if my dad knocked down a stack of milk bottles with a softball. I had loved Spuds from the moment I saw the bull terrier Bud Light mascot in a Superbowl commercial. But when Dad knocked over all the bottles, the carny refused to award me the doll. Maybe he had made a big promise so that my dad would play. Maybe he hadn't expected him to win. This cruel reversal knocked the joy right out of me. "You're gonna take away a prize from a little girl?" Dad yelled. A crowd gathered. "Forget it, let's just leave," Mom said. But Dad let everyone know just how much of a liar the carny was, and the carny stopped Dad from running off business by negotiating a framed 5x7 photograph of Spuds. That photo hung on my wall until the day I moved out, a reminder to stand up to people who did me wrong.

• • •

I started life in a single-wide trailer. I don't remember much from that time. Mom says we ate a lot of boxed mac and cheese dinners and that if it weren't for my mamaw and papaw, who used Mamaw's employee discount at K-mart, I wouldn't have had many clothes. Looking through the photo albums, I wouldn't know we struggled. All I see is a chunky, happy baby.

My mom had worked since she was fifteen, everywhere from a bakery to a Ramada Inn, where she was a housekeeper, and at factories where she sawed wood, operated a riveter, and tested car ignitions. When I was born, my parents decided she would become a stay-at-home mom while my dad worked for the county roads department, one of the ten manual labor jobs he had over the course of six years. Four years later, he found a job like none other when he became a bingo salesman.

"Your dad does what?" kids always asked with puppy-dog head tilts. "Like the game old people play? How does he earn money doing that?" Most of my classmates' parents worked at the factories, the county hospital, out of an eighteen-wheeler, or on the family farm. Their jobs were familiar and didn't evoke too many questions. Explaining my dad's job wasn't easy, and not everyone approved of his work. My Methodist missionary great-grandmother certainly didn't. Not even my grandfather, who lived the life of a sailor years after he left the Navy, liked the idea of his son selling bingo supplies. Despite the company's exclusive devotion to charitable fundraising, bingo was gambling. Few people understood how anyone could make an honest living at it. "It's not very Christian," I've been told. The only thing most people knew about the industry was from some national news story about racketeering, which fueled the assumption that all charitable bingo was a mask for corruption.

Dad's job was fun for me. In the summers, I rode with him on his route through Columbus. His customers regularly filled my arms with pop and candy. And I loved playing in his box truck. Packed with colorful daubers, animated tickets, and prize baskets filled with chocolates, I likened it to a board game on wheels. My favorite thing was searching for pull-tab tickets that had fallen out of boxes. Pull-tabs are paper tickets with symbols, like diamonds or stars, hidden behind perforated tabs. I'd sit on the tailgate, legs swinging, peeling back the tabs in hopes of revealing a winning combination, pretending to win big money.

As much as I loved that truck, I also hated it because every other week it took my dad to Cincinnati, where he spent three nights away from home. Dad being away was an adjustment for our family. He didn't like leaving us, and we had a greater sense of security when he was at home. But after he earned more in his first week than he had over the course of eight weeks at his previous job at the county roads department, my parents decided that it was worth it. Better income meant they could provide me with an upbringing different from theirs, a life where I wouldn't have to decide where or with whom I would live or worry about what I would eat.

The longer Dad drove the bingo truck, the more my parents' finances improved, as did our quality of life. A year later, my sister, Mattie, was born. We enjoyed a full refrigerator. Mom paid off layaways more easily, and my parents began eliminating debt. Dad bought Mom a necklace. And they vacationed for the first time since their honeymoon.

While some things changed, my parents remained the same honest, down-to-earth people. They took us out to eat more, mostly to Pizza Hut and, when they felt fancy, Olive Garden, but Mom still cooked most of our meals. She worked hard raising us girls, managing her household and land, and serving as my homeroom mother, field trip chaperone, and Girl Scout troop leader. My parents still wore out the knees of their jeans. They still spent an entire day mowing, pausing to drink from the garden hose. And Dad still complained that the house looked like New York City when we turned on more than three lights. Then he turned off two to lower the electricity bill.

It wasn't only their practicality that made them down-to-earth. They cared about other people. Although Dad's job expanded their social spheres, I never saw them ditch old friends for new ones. They told me that when you care about people you show up in their lives, especially when they need support, because sooner or later everyone needs support. I listened in as they spent hours on the front porch swing, comforting friends in abusive relationships and wrecked marriages. I saw them donate trash bags of clothes to neighbors. They fed and transported kids who didn't have supportive families. And they attended the funerals of their friends' parents and the ballgames of their friends' kids, even when they hadn't seen those friends in years. They're still at it today, but you wouldn't know because you won't see them doing it, and they won't tell you.

• • •

I'm grateful to have grown up in a loving home with generous, hardworking parents who are still together today. They were the reason I was confident in school and became a leader in my community. Maybe that sounds a little weird. Most stories about being bullied aren't told by the confident kids. But the stability I knew didn't mean the ground never shook. My parents argued, mostly because of Dad's mood and about finances. As they gained money, they also lost money learning how to manage assets and liabilities. When unforeseen expenses arose, Dad resisted tapping into savings, even when Mom reminded him that was the purpose of their savings. Instead, he worked even harder to earn more, which created pressure. After a day spent drenched on the loading docks, climbing in and out of his truck hundreds of times, he spent evenings belly-down, recruiting me to walk on his injured back. His pain combined with his full-throttle work ethic sometimes made for tense dinners.

Not everyone handles the transition from work to home in the same way. When I have a stressful day, I unload it on my husband as soon as I walk through the door so I get it all out, and he knows my mood has nothing to do with him. I think that comes from seeing Dad hold his bad days in. Dad tried to keep work at work. He didn't talk about what he had been through because he didn't want to put that on us. And he wasn't the type who decompressed in front of *Wheel of Fortune* with a glass of wine. He had to do something with all that emotion, like grab a shovel and work on the land. If he didn't release that energy, he ended up doing what he tried not to do, which was yelling at us.

He'd stomp through the door, snapping, and I'd react by mouthing off and mocking his body language. Mom would yell back, telling him that if he was going to take work out on us, he needed to go back to work. Sometimes he would. More often, he'd go outside and do yard work. He'd return calmer, but for the next day or two Mom would give him the silent treatment to let him know just how angry she was.

When Mattie was a teenager, she coined the term "monkey" to describe Dad's seemingly unprovoked anger—his deep sighs at the dinner table and forceful forking of his food, scowling, and curtness. "Dad's getting monkey," she would say as a warning to Mom and me and as a way of calling him out. Mattie knew how to get through to Dad in ways I couldn't. The more she pointed out his behavior, the more self-aware he became, until one day he danced around like a chimpanzee at a birthday party.

Eventually, he learned how to relax, but to this day, whenever one of us girls senses a moment coming on, we remind him, "Don't get monkey," which helps defuse tension and holds all of us accountable for our behavior.

When I get fired up, I, too, have to do something with all of that emotion. Looking back at how I handled my problems in school, I realize I combined my parents' responses to arguments into my own blow-up-stomp-away-ignore technique, which expressed my anger effectively but solved my problems poorly.

Over the years, I've learned how to release. I pray, exercise, write, or perform chores, but sometimes I still need help calming my monkey, which is why I'm thankful for my mellow husband who gently calls me out and guides me with logical thinking.

3. MONEY MINDSETS

AS MY PARENTS LEARNED more about money, they argued less and used it to grow. Every Saturday morning at the kitchen table, Dad conducted a brainstorming session, jotting plans on a yellow legal pad. Once he got everything out of his head, he asked Mom to sit with him to discuss bills, tasks, tithes, and dreams. Instead of accepting, "We can't afford it," they evaluated, "Should we afford it?" and, if so, "How can we afford it?" When ideas changed, crumpled paper balls littered the floor. Failure lasted no longer than the pen rest.

I imitated their actions, making wish and chore lists, from which they taught me how to negotiate. I learned I wouldn't earn money for every task, and that just because I earned money didn't mean I should spend it. I also learned that I didn't get everything just because I wanted it and we had money to buy it—like the jelly sandals I pleaded for summer after summer. When I earned a new toy, I understood my parents reserved the right to revoke it should I misbehave. Because I saw my parents toss spare change in a can, I did the same. When they granted me money to go out with my friends, I spent conservatively and always returned their change. And from the time I was twelve years old, my parents encouraged my entrepreneurship in babysitting, baking, car detailing, and teaching basketball skills to kids. To this day, my family knows I'm the one who stretches a dollar the furthest. I think I do that because, at just the right age, I noticed the shift in my parents' finances, which caused me to respect the process of earning money and the power of what it could do.

Having been on both sides of struggle and stability, I now understand why some people squirm at the mention of money while others talk about it as casually as what they ate for lunch. How we're raised to think about money can affect our entire lives and how we interact with others. In my youth, as my parents became more relaxed discussing money, I grew comfortable talking about it too. However, I was also taught how important it was that I only talked about it at home. Outside our walls, it was best to keep quiet.

• • •

Where I come from, we don't mention money unless we talk about what we can't afford. We tend to associate money with greed because many of us learn, per the misquoting of 1 Timothy 6:10, that money is the root of all evil. While money is often misused, our demonizing it blinds us to the truth of the verse, that the love of money, not money itself, is a root of all kinds of evil. Money is simply a tool that reveals the heart's intentions. Like a hammer, it only impacts when you swing it. With it you can cause destruction, or you can build a house. But no matter your generosity, if money provides you opportunities that others don't have, some people will take swings to bust you up.

When I was growing up in my county of over a hundred thousand people, the median household income was $31,284. Only 10 percent of the population earned above $50,000. I knew at least one other classmate whose dad worked in sales. I assumed he earned an above-average paycheck because he traveled internationally. And there were rumors that some of the boys came from wealthy farming families. But those families and most of the families I knew didn't seem more well-to-do than any of the others. I didn't think of my family any differently, but the remarks of some adults or their children toward us caused me to wonder if they thought otherwise.

"You don't deserve so much."

"You're taking another vacation?"

"Must be nice to have another new car."

"Your kids are so spoiled."

"They're such snobs."

"It's easy for you."

Those are just some of the things I heard thrown around about us or toward us.

Although I enjoyed some nice things in my youth, I remember when a boy made fun of me in fifth grade when Dad drove me to school in a car with rusted-out floorboards and a loud muffler. I don't remember feeling embarrassed to ride in that car. It was neat watching the road pass beneath my feet. I didn't even consider much wrong with it until the boy laughed and asked, "Who would drive a beat-up old car like that?" Years before, my mom and this boy's dad had worked together at a factory, so I didn't understand why he thought he was above my car, and I didn't like his judgment. He didn't know how much that car meant to my dad. His grandparents, who had since passed, had gifted it to him for his high school graduation. I'll never forget Dad standing in the driveway with his back turned toward me as he watched it towed to the scrap yard. He stood there for a minute after it disappeared, wiping his face. As I recall that scene and think about the things I've watched leave my life, I realize he must've felt like more than a hunk of metal was being hauled away. At that point in life, though, rather than inform the boy of these things, I just wanted to shut him up. "Yours is worse," I said, and he agreed.

Maybe it was easier to feel like I fit in with my peers in a school where 99 percent of us were white and middle-class. But I now see that there were also differences that made lasting impressions on me. Like any other school, mine had cliques: farmers, athletes, marching band, and skaters. Students crossed over, and I don't remember anyone making a big deal about it. However, I do remember kids hassling others by calling them preps, which meant they acted like they were better than everyone because they dressed in name brands. Most of us were of the same economic class, but we still knew who was at the top and who was at the bottom. One of my skater friends once told me, "Tami, you're a prep, but you're not like the others."

"What's that supposed to mean?" I said, unsure whether I should be offended.

"That you wear Abercrombie, but you don't act like it," she said. "You're nice."

I remember it so well because I appreciated that she saw through outer appearances and into my heart. She didn't hold my brand-new sweater against me, and I didn't hold her hand-me-down Grateful Dead T-shirt against her.

As much as I felt like I was just another rural route kid from Map-Dot America, I now look back and see ways I was different. One thing that set me apart was Dad's job.

When a boy claimed my dad was a mobster, I tried explaining how bingo games raised money for schools to purchase new playground equipment. If only I could make him understand the good that came from my dad's work, like the sports organizations that provided kids with pathways out of poverty, the rescue foundation that saved thousands of neglected pets, the fraternal clubs that supported veterans and their families, and the volunteer fire departments that purchased new equipment to better serve their communities. But he only wanted to bring to life what he had watched in some old-time gangster movie. "Selling bingo supplies isn't a real job," he said. "No way is that legit."

I was about to kick his tipped chair and watch his butt hit the floor when a girl in the back of the classroom interrupted. "Don't ever be ashamed of what your dad does for a living," she said. "Mine's a garbageman."

Although some people judged my dad's job, I don't ever remember feeling ashamed of it. There were certain ticket themes that I didn't like, and Dad sometimes had to deal with sketchy businessmen, but I didn't focus on the negatives. I was proud to have a dad who worked hard to provide for our family and who loved his customers and their causes. To this day, whenever I feel the need to defend my dad's job, I hear the girl from the back of the classroom, reminding me that I don't have to convince those who aren't willing to listen.

Another thing that set me apart was my house. Most of the kids I grew up with lived in old farmhouses, manufactured homes, quaint 1950s Cape Cods, and 1960s-style ranches. And one of my best friends lived in one of those grand Victorian homes built during the oil boom. But no one had a house quite like mine.

My eighteen-hundred-square-foot log cabin was unique not by design but because of miscommunications between my parents and the builders. By the time they discovered the mistakes, it was too costly to make changes. While my parents cringed over irregular staircases, openings that were supposed to be walls, and crooked pictures hanging on uneven log walls that were supposed to be drywall, everyone else, including me, looked around with fascination.

My house was in the country, down a long driveway, nestled into a grove of white pines. Under a vaulted ceiling, two forty-foot beams spanned the great room (those were supposed to be there). They beckoned the attention of anyone who walked through the door. When my friends came over, their eyes widened as they touched the walls like they were in some fairytale cabin in the forest. "Careful. Don't get a splinter," I would say, knowing how quickly imagination could become a reality.

I only knew of two other kids whose families had built houses, and no one I knew lived in a log cabin—or had a swimming pool. My friends knew my house as a fun place for many reasons. They loved my mom's cooking, Dad's loud music, my cats and dogs, and adventuring through our woods. We had board games, a basketball hoop, and an air hockey table. We could always find something to do. There weren't too many times anyone turned down an invitation to come over. I enjoyed sharing the things I had with a wide range of friends. But when I think about the nickname some of my classmates gave me my senior year, it gives me reason to believe that what I had and how I got it was a big part of why I was bullied.

Whether my family struggled, thrived, or something in between, I resented people who dissed who we were and what we had. Why couldn't they see us like I saw us and support us, or at least keep their mouths shut? Perhaps some people encapsulated Dad in youth—as many of us do with people from our hometowns. Maybe they thought that someone with his temper needed to be humbled or wasn't capable of changing. Maybe they thought that because his grandparents had provided things like a new car, he had had enough handed to him and didn't deserve more. Maybe that kind of thinking played into them labeling me and my sister as spoiled when they saw us with something new. Or maybe peoples' rude comments had less to do with him and our family and more to do with their overall mindset toward others.

Sometimes it doesn't matter who you are, what you have, or how you arrived where you are. Some people put others down to make themselves feel better because they only focus on what others have, or more accurately, what they don't have themselves. They believe another person's gain means their loss because there aren't enough opportunities, money, love, friendship, or happiness to go around. They lie in wait to capitalize on others' flaws. If something hasn't been done, they'll say it can't be done. Once it's achieved, they'll tell you why it won't last, why the outcome is unfair, or they will discredit the accomplishment by squawking your unworthiness all over town.

I used to think that if people really knew my family, they wouldn't pass judgment. I have learned, though, that nothing protects any of us from criticism. And as much as I hate feeling judged, I cringe at the thought of how many times I've done it to others when I feel attacked. It's my gut reaction to meanness, a reaction that was heightened after I was bullied. It's one of the many reasons why I need Jesus. The closer I stay to Him, the softer my heart. The softer my heart, the more aware I am of how my limited perspective blocks me from seeing the whole picture, like when my classmate couldn't see beyond a rusted car. This is my cue to ask God to help me change how I view offense. Instead of reacting with opinions, I ask questions that help me better understand myself, others, and why we hurt each other. Those questions remind me that we humans just don't know what we don't know, and sometimes we concern ourselves with things that are none of our business.

While in younger days my parents confronted critics, when I was a kid, I saw them handle beauty salon chatter with grace. Initially, they might have seethed privately, but the more they disregarded backbiting the sooner it dissolved. If anything, it drove them back to the kitchen table with a yellow legal pad. I, however, did not extend the same grace, and it would eventually land me in the most trouble I had ever been in.

4. HOOP AND HALOS

THE FIRST TIME I REMEMBER caring about what others thought about me was in kindergarten on Olympic Day. When I received my ribbons—all reds and one blue—the two cutest and most athletic boys laughed, pointing out the inferiority of my awards compared to another girl's all blues and one red. My tears simmered with competitiveness, but not against the girl who beat me. With girls, I hopscotched. My best friends, Annie and Dawn, and I never played for a prize, just for fun, which safeguarded our feelings. But boys competed for a serious outcome. Boys were the enemies, back before hormones played a role, and because they challenged me, I set out to prove myself against them.

Olympic Day carried over to gym class, where I matched them by climbing to the top of the cargo net. At lunch, I arm-wrestled and chugged chocolate milk against them. In music class, I sang just as loudly. I earned star stickers on my tests and made honor roll every quarter like them. At recess, I raced from the blacktop to the fence. I kicked a soccer ball just as far. And if I took an elbow to the teeth underneath the basketball hoop, the pain was worth the rush of conquering them.

As the boys grew, they whooped me (and any other girl who dared them) harder. Occasionally, during Red Rover, one of us girls broke through the boys' arms, but more often we dropped like sparrows flying into windows. When the boys taunted Dawn, who lay gasping for breath, Annie and I snapped. The rest of the girls followed as we hooked arms and charged toward our rivals with the boldest courage ever displayed on that grass field. Our chain didn't always protect us from our stronger opponents, but our bruises bolstered our allegiance to each other.

• • •

When my girlfriends started playing in the co-ed basketball league, I joined too. Dad also tried something new, volunteering as my team's coach. Halfway through my first practice, I vowed to quit. While the boys dribbled with control, I bounced the ball off my foot every step. They laughed. I fumed, speckling the court with droplets of inadequacy.

Giving up would not fly with my parents. Dad dedicated his evenings to coaching me in our basement, where he showed me how to control the ball with my fingertips instead of smacking it with my palm. Not every practice flowed smoothly. When we matched impatience, Mom called timeouts. As our behind-the-scenes coach, she knew just when to tiptoe downstairs to give us the eyeball. Her gentleness paired with Dad's tough love encouraged me. Within weeks I dribbled with the boys, and my family huddled around my team and me.

Not only did Dad serve as our coach, Mom became a scorekeeper and the concession manager, Mattie was our team's reluctant cheerleader, and we recruited my best friend, Kevin, to join our team. Kevin and I were more like brother and sister. We met when we were three years old, when he moved in next door with his mom, who married my uncle Dave. I couldn't have had a better teammate.

Kevin and I spent our childhood swinging on grapevines, rolling down hills in cardboard boxes, and stranding ourselves on a raft in the middle of the pond. After swashbuckling across fourteen acres, we sprayed water from the hose over each other's briar-scratched legs. We picked gravel out of each other's knees and soothed our bee stings with cherry popsicles. I still can't believe neither of us broke a bone, especially Kevin, who wrecked his bike and tripped over stumps more times than I could count.

Kevin's lack of coordination wasn't his fault. Uncle Dave, older than the average dad, didn't often play tag or throw a baseball with him. Instead, Kevin learned movement alongside my family and me. That's how we noticed his athleticism and persuaded him to join our team. Kevin got one of his best friends, Johnny, to play, which scored our team the two tallest boys in our grade. All they had to do to grab a rebound was reach over the other players.

Our team became like extended family. My parents transported kids whose parents worked third shift or weren't involved. And some teammates spent the night at our house before games to ensure they were well fed and on time. Boys I once rivaled became my allies as we defended each other on the playground. I never worried about a boy bullying me because Kevin, Johnny, and my other teammates would yell at them. And I would do the same for them, if needed.

Helping each other off the court strengthened our dynamic on the court. No one player dominated our team. We were taught that each of us played roles that contributed to our chances of winning, a lesson not easily applied.

In practice, when we didn't pay attention or bickered like siblings, we faced frozen push-ups. Just before our chests touched the floor, we held the push up until our coaches said stop. The more we blamed each other, or complained, or quit, the longer our punishment. We understood we had two choices: spend the rest of practice under the confinement of a stopwatch or change our attitudes and play. Like most kids, we responded to structure.

"Come on, we can do this!" we said, echoing our coaches' support. Or to the teammate with the shakiest arms, "Keep going! We're almost done!" In our weaknesses, we discovered we could control our reactions by employing what our coaches called "mental toughness," an essential tool in games.

Our team played just within the rules. If we weren't allowed in a space, we played at the edge of that space. When an opponent failed to protect the ball, we snatched that sucker like monkeys invading a picnic. We ran unexpected patterns and caused distractions, which made some people accuse us of cheating.

"She's trying to hurt my son!" said a mother as she stomped toward a referee to complain about my defense. When parents yelled about our play, we didn't understand that their criticism pertained less to us and more to their emotions, bias, or lack of understanding of the game. Those were the times our coaches pulled us into a huddle and reminded us, "Play like we practiced."

The resiliency I developed from frozen push-ups helped me overcome distractions my entire life. It's what pushed me through the Grand Canyon on a twenty-four-mile rim-to-rim hike when the last site of water access closed unexpectedly. Ascending the final five miles, I wanted to surrender to my parched throat. Instead, step by step, as my quarter-sized blisters rubbed against my boots, I spoke encouragement until I reached the top.

When my husband and I suffered 105-degree fevers and lost twenty pounds each in four days on our honeymoon, mental toughness dragged us out of Mexico to seek proper medical treatment for E. coli.

Mental toughness helped me stay calm when my small business received a fifteen-thousand-dollar tax bill I wasn't prepared to pay. Mental toughness is choosing happiness when I don't feel like it. It's forging a plan instead of freaking out. The ability to persevere under pressure is a fundamental element of success, something I learned as the stakes increased.

On my all-girl Amateur Athletic Union (AAU) team, I encountered fierce competition. Unlike the school season, referees let us play through jersey jerks and shoves. Physicality was only half the challenge. If a competitor could get into your head, she could beat you no matter your skill.

At the foul line, I blocked out opponents who tried to convince me I'd miss my shot. I accepted smack-talk as part of the game, but when players crossed that boundary, I couldn't ignore their actions. In one game, when I fell on the floor, a girl stood on my ponytail. I yelled and swung my fist at her ankle, but she didn't budge until my teammates moved her. On another occasion, as I sprinted down the court, an opponent clotheslined me, sending me to the hospital on a stretcher. Although I encountered a few dirty players, no aggressive game made me consider all girls mean. My AAU teammates proved otherwise.

Every summer, we left our barn-bolted backboards to travel thousands of miles, playing up to eight games per weekend in sweltering gymnasiums. We shared meals and hotel rooms, prayers and pool parties, all the while nurturing our chemistry. Without words, we knew how to lift each other at just the right moment. When we doubted our jellified legs could run another sprint, a hand extended. We pressed on, refusing to disappoint one another because we played for more than trophies.

Not only my teammates strengthened my perception of girls. Players from a top-ranked team proved competitors don't have to be enemies. In the state tournament, we vied for one of three top spots in the state with a well-established dynasty of girls from prestigious schools, whose fathers played professional football. When they entered the gym—matching bags strapped across erect shoulders—and claimed the bleachers two rows below us, assumption stirred our insecurities.

"Who do they think they are?" we said. "They're trying to intimidate us."

We sounded ridiculous.

"Why don't you go talk to them?" said our coaches.

Stomping down the bleachers, we intended to expose the girls' arrogance, only to disprove ourselves. We learned about each other, traded scouting reports on a team neither of us liked, and exchanged phone numbers. That year they placed second, earning a trip to nationals. We placed fourth, one spot away from qualifying, let down but rooting for our new friends.

It never felt natural to congratulate opponents for the wins I wanted myself, but because my parents talked to me about healthy competition, I discovered that acknowledging another girl's strengths didn't lessen mine. I could help a girl off the floor no matter the color of her jersey. In every part of life, I wanted to surround myself with others who embraced that kind of sportsmanship. But no matter where the competition occurred, not everyone played the game the same way or called timeouts to take an honest look at how their actions affected others.

• • •

When I was six, I wrote on my mamaw's pristine white table runner. Paralyzed by the ink line, my quietness attracted suspicion.

"Did you do that?" she said.

At the exact moment of my denial, I noticed my grip on the evidence. Forever imprinted on me is that sweet woman's disappointment. She deserved the truth. And I realized I would've suffered far less if I came clean when called out.

I knew better, having learned from my parents and a Ten Commandments book on a table in our living room. In an illustration of "Thou shall not give false testimony against your neighbor" (Exodus 20:16), a soldier towered over a pleading mother as he held a sword to her infant. Another woman snuck away, smirking. It wasn't clear who this woman was, but I was sure her lie had resulted in the baby's death. Every time I turned to the image, I grew more repulsed by the woman, until one day I could no longer look at her, so I scratched out her eyeballs with a penny. Maybe I saw myself in her. I just knew I never wanted to be like her. Lying hurt people, which hurt me.

Church seemed like the last place I'd witness lying, but sometimes even teammates clothesline each other. One evening, I overheard two moms talking about Miss Sally, our youth choir director. "It isn't right she keeps the doors closed," one woman said. "Parents should be allowed in there."

"She's probably teaching witchcraft," the other mom said.

I don't know why Miss Sally closed the doors, perhaps to keep her critics at bay. Was she really a witch? Mom didn't think so. They were friends. Nothing about Miss Sally made me question her faith. She played Mary in the Christmas pageant, rocked babies in the nursery, and washed dishes after chicken noodle dinners. I still don't know if the rumor was true, but it spread, and like a great forest set on fire by a small spark (James 3:5), Miss Sally's reputation burned, set ablaze by loose lips. A month later she left the church, and I left the choir.

The rumor revealed a power play. As decision-makers gained more authority, similar incidents happened to others, including my parents.

"Why's he glaring at us?" I said about a church elder, unaware that my parents had declined positions that he had appointed them to without their consent. After that, the guy wouldn't even return Dad's salutation from across the gas pump.

Although the Bible warned against unkindness, I never remember action taken to address it amongst our members. Perhaps the pastor confronted people privately, or maybe I missed that sermon. Why couldn't grown-ups form a game plan like my basketball team, where no one person prevailed but everyone fulfilled their unique roles for the betterment of the team? Some people didn't seem happy unless they dominated all the plays. Gradually, our congregation fractured.

Rather than battle these social powers, my family devoted Sundays to basketball. And although we never wavered from our convictions, we disengaged from church for the next nine years.

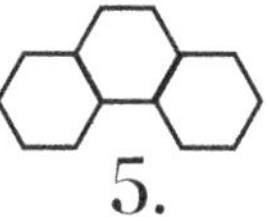

5.
BEHIND THE OAK TREE

THERE'S NO NEED TO SHOVE anyone into a locker when words—even subtle body language—do just as much damage. No matter our age, people manipulate relationships to gain power. It's the type of bullying that often goes undetected, and it can happen anywhere—amongst families and friends, in the workplace, at church, and on social media. Still, we tend to associate that kind of bullying with kids, maybe because so many of us can recall the wounds inflicted on us in school as if they happened yesterday.

My yesterday goes back to fifth grade, when students from my district's two elementary schools merged into one middle school. On the first day, I rushed to the blacktop hoops, where the elbows of older, stronger boys pushed me toward the monkey bars.

I wished Bailey was there. We had been friends since the first day of second grade. Tears had streamed down her cheeks. "She's new here," said our teacher. "She could use a friend." So I put my arm around her and showed her she didn't need to be scared. But Bailey had moved away, and now I had to take my own advice.

I scanned the field for friends from my old playground. Kevin and Johnny were playing football, and although I was a tomboy, I never gravitated toward the game. Annie and Dawn pumped their legs on the swings, but the other swings were taken. They had grown closer that summer. We were all still friends, but I knew they were each other's best friend and felt like I needed a best friend of my own. So, I headed toward some familiar faces who were whacking a tetherball.

Day after day, I returned to the safety of the tetherball pole with the same girls. There, all of us learned who was whom and how everyone was connected. That's where I met Rylan, who gained my respect when she confronted boys who tried to break the string from the pole, pinching their arms all the way to a teacher. As much as Rylan punished the boys when they teased her, they loved her. She was a natural beauty, even when her face reddened.

The tetherball pole is also where I met Sara. Across the playground, she and her friends bounced into a flag football game, where Sara outran the fastest player, flaunting his flag like a perfume-spritzed hankie.

"Everyone's friends with Sara," Rylan said.

"Why doesn't she come over here and play, then?" I asked.

"I don't know," Rylan said. "Someone go ask her."

One of the other-side girls skipped across the field. Just like that, Sara and her friends began visiting our tetherball pole, and my friends and I joined their cheerleading dances. Within weeks, Sara and I exchanged best-friends-forever necklaces. If only I had known the reason those charms looked like a broken heart.

I likened Sara to my babysitters. Her authority demanded my attention. "Let's go over there," she said. "Do it like this." She taught me the "We Must Increase Our Bust" song and how to play MASH, which influenced whom we associated with in real life. She introduced me to padded underwire bras, name-brand jeans, shaving, and cappuccino. She was the first girl I knew who took bathroom breaks to dab her face with a powder-puff.

The need for these things intrigued me. The only time I spent more than a couple minutes looking at myself in the mirror was to see if I had stained a cherry Kool-Aid mustache to my lip. Sara told me Kool-Aid mustaches weren't cool. She pressured me to cut my hair because, she said, "It would look prettier if you cut it short like mine." She smacked my hand when I chewed my nails and taught me how to cross my legs to hide cellulite. In middle school, looks mattered because boys mattered.[1]

I knew how to impress the guys with my jump shot, but when it came to Sara's discussions about boys, we weren't playing the same game. Who knew kissing had anything to do with bases? I had never even had a boyfriend, only crushes where we merely said we liked each other and exchanged an extra piece of candy with our Valentines. Every time I revealed one of my secret crushes to Sara, she became his girlfriend a few days later. I never even knew we liked the same boys. Because Sara always chose the games we played, I felt bossed around and deceived when she changed the rules midway. My friends and I didn't act this way toward one another, but what could I do? What Sara wanted, Sara got—boys, friends, hula hoops, and all.

My only option was to keep quiet and tag along to the oak tree just beyond the boundary of our schoolyard. There, Sara invested only in me. We whispered and giggled about cute boys, girls we didn't like, and a friend of hers who sucked his thumb. Whenever anyone interrupted, she shouted, "You can't come back here."

"Yeah. This is private," I would say, emboldened by her brazenness.

Recesses later, the secrets we shared behind the tree branched onto the playground, twisting further from their origin. The more I got pulled into arguments amongst different circles and called into the guidance counselor's office, the more I noticed how Sara interacted with others differently than I did and the less I wanted to be her friend. Behind the oak tree, her remarks about people didn't match how she treated them in person. If I didn't like someone, I addressed them the same way I talked about them behind the tree. I obeyed the don't-run-your-mouth-if-you-aren't-willing-to-fight philosophy. I didn't look for trouble, but if I faced a problem, I confronted it similarly to how I played ball—with pressure defense so I could regain possession and score. I no longer trusted Sara with my secrets, but how could I ever reject a girl so highly regarded?

Sara and I visited the oak tree once more. After we sent away Melissa, my friend since kindergarten, I gulped and told Sara, "That wasn't nice."

"It's no big deal," she said. "She'll get over it."

"I don't wanna come back here anymore." I bolted for the swings, Sara followed, and we resumed our activities.

The next day on the playground, a few other-side girls rushed to me. "Sara said you called Melissa a bitch." Melissa joined the huddle, followed by Dawn, Annie, and Rylan.

"I didn't call you that, Melissa. I stood up for you."

"That's not what Sara said."

I could no longer allow Sara to get away with lying. I had to call her out, like when my mamaw caught me writing on her table. Marching across the field like gangbusters, I interrupted Sara's game of kickball. "Stop telling lies," I said.

"What are you talking about?" she said.

"You said I called Melissa a bitch. You know I didn't," I said, wagging my finger in her face. "We're not friends anymore."

With reclaimed spunk, I headed to the basketball court and demanded to play, favoring skinned knees over offense.

Had I fully comprehended my mamaw's lesson, I would've remembered the fever-like flush on my cheeks as I struggled to look at her. She didn't raise her voice, call my mom into the room, or send me to stand in the corner. Instead, she seasoned her disappointment with grace, which is why, after three denials, I finally admitted my guilt and secretly vowed to never lie to her again. If I had extended the same mercy to Sara, maybe everything would've turned out differently. But I never considered how confronting her in front of our friends made her feel or how it would affect us. I never even questioned whether Sara had spread the rumor or if Melissa retaliated by instigating it herself. My pre-adolescent brain only focused on feeling fed up and acting. To everyone watching, I marked a line in the pea gravel. The playground was never the same.

• • •

In a class of one hundred fifty students, the two most competitive girls couldn't simply disagree and go separate ways. Sara and

I were adamant about controlling our relationship in our own styles. When I was angry, I typically responded in one of two ways: go off or shutdown. Either way, the message was, "Don't cross me because I'll never talk to you again." I thought my silent treatment toward Sara sent a clear message that I wanted nothing to do with her any longer. Like basketball, I thought the game was over, and that was that. But our "game" never ended, because we saw each other every day at school. Ignoring Sara only deepened our conflict by shutting down her ability to proactively participate. Meanwhile, Sara subtly spit her resentment into everyone else's lunch milk to create empathy and regain control.[2]

"See how Tami's sitting at that table?" she said to our classmates. "She won't be my friend 'cause she hates me."

Although I didn't want to be friends with Sara and I called her names when she angered me, I didn't hate her. I wasn't allowed to say I hated someone. It was one of my mom's biggest no-nos. Hating someone was like wishing death on them, and I didn't want that. I just wanted Sara to leave me alone. I didn't understand why Sara thought this. Maybe it was her way of trying to understand my attitudes and actions or win our fight. Neither did I get why our classmates believed the things she said. Now, as I consider how the two of us behaved toward one another, I see how we nurtured our rivalry and supported our peers' inflexible notions.

Sara knew my weaknesses. She had seen my temper surface when people called me names and told lies about me, like the time she and her friends said another girl ran her mouth about me, and without question I sent that girl somersaulting. Even if she had called me a name, my action was uncalled for. I knew it immediately, and the other girls made sure I knew it, yelling at me until I yelled back. Only one girl knew just how much the girl I pushed annoyed me. I had told Sara behind the oak tree. Sara knew I always reacted, and she targeted my vulnerability.[3]

When I asked why she lied, she would say she hadn't. Every time I pointed out her behavior, she flipped things around and blamed me for doing the same thing she had done to me. I'd blow up, while Sara said to her friends, "I don't know why she's so mad." As this scenario became repetitious, classmates viewed our disputes as a result of my inability to control my anger and competition. I always took the blame because I confronted Sara and never stuck around to make amends. Sara did this to irritate me without anyone questioning her, which became a valuable tool to control our conflict as we headed into adolescence.[4]

6.

NICE GIRLS FINISH FIRST

SARA WASN'T THE ONLY GIRL I had problems with. In fifth grade, Chelsea moved to our school, like a flame searching for a fuse. Before I ever met her, I heard she liked my boyfriend, Ethan, and that she had been telling people that Laney Johnson had called me easy. No one messed with Laney. She was known for back talking teachers and fist-fighting. I didn't want on her bad side. When I told my parents they called Chelsea's mom, who wasn't interested in addressing the problem. The principal and guidance counselor set up a conversation between me and Laney and explained the situation. "I didn't call you that," Laney said. Even the principal believed her. If Laney Johnson called someone a name, she wasn't going to take it back. She'd badmouth that person all the way into a detention.

"I'm glad," I said. "Because I don't want to make you mad."

The principal promised to talk to Chelsea and gave us orders not to deal with her ourselves.

After that, Laney and I talked more than we had before, and I realized she wasn't as scary as I had previously thought. We never had a problem with each other again.

Chelsea continued telling everyone I was promiscuous, which caused problems between me and Ethan in seventh grade. When he started cutting our conversations short, I marched to Chelsea's locker in between class periods. "Stop telling lies about me," I demanded. She brushed me off, walking away at the sound of the bell.

Confronting her seemed to fuel her, because it only took a few weeks before Ethan broke up with me in the hallway before a dance. Perhaps he was worried about what others thought, but I was more concerned with what he thought. "How can you believe her over me?" I yelled. He knew we had only held hands and kissed. I told him I didn't like anyone else, but he shrugged his shoulders and walked away.

I ran to the restroom, where Bailey found me wiping my eyes. Bailey had moved back that year, and we instantly resumed our friendship. When the door swung open, I was relieved it was her and not Chelsea. I let my tears fall. Bailey put her arm around me like I did with her the first day of second grade. She waved in some girls, who searched their bags for tissues and my face for the story.

Outside the gymnasium, the girls gathered around me, giving me pep talks about how I didn't need that jerk. I entered bopping, determined to show Ethan I could have fun without him. But two songs later, I ended up back in the hallway, surrounded by tissues, after seeing him and Chelsea slow dancing.

When Mom picked me up, I told her what had happened. My parents contacted the principal, who called me and Chelsea to his office the following week. "What's going on between you two?" he said.

"She's telling lies about me," I snapped.

Chelsea denied everything. I boiled. I failed to convince the principal that she was the devil. He held up his hands to stop us. "Okay, tell each other you're sorry and let's not have this kind of meeting again," he said. We muttered half-hearted apologies, but I wasn't sorry. When I got home, I hung her picture on my dartboard and honed my skill at throwing bull's-eyes.

I wished I could've ignored Chelsea into oblivion, but no matter how much she aggravated me, I found a way to tolerate her because we were basketball teammates.

Chelsea often used the intimacy of our team to collect information, spread rumors, and create conflict. Our freshman year, she burst into the locker room, asking all of us, "Did you hear about Gina?" Gina and Chelsea were friends until they clashed. "Her boyfriend got arrested for shoplifting a pregnancy test." The room erupted, and I joined the prodding.

Within an hour people approached me, saying Gina wanted to fight. I had no desire to fight her, but I wanted to clear up the confusion. I met Gina in the hallway, where a crowd surrounded and urged us against each other.

"Chelsea said you're spreading lies about me because you hate me and want me to go to jail with my boyfriend."

"Chelsea told you what?"

"My boyfriend didn't even go to jail."

"I never said he did. Chelsea did. Where is she?"

No one knew. As usual, she had instigated a fight and disappeared. I pushed through the crowd and returned to practice. Chelsea slipped in late, right when Coach started talking. I gave her a death stare, but she wouldn't look at me, so I passed the ball to her extra hard, hoping to hear her finger pop. I swore to keep my mouth shut around her, but my disengagement wouldn't solve much. She awaited any moment she could twist to make me look bad.

During a game in which our rival outmatched us, Coach sent in a substitute for me. On the bench, I carelessly tossed my water bottle behind me, which squirted an opposing fan. "Watch it, ya sore loser!" he said.

"Sorry. I didn't mean to," I said.

Chelsea whipped around when she heard the man complain. "I can't believe you doused him," she said. Another teammate, who also had her back to the incident, joined the scolding.

"You guys didn't even see what happened," I said. They grumbled, and I rolled my eyes.

After the game, Chelsea provoked our teammates, dwelling on what she portrayed as my poor leadership qualities. Suddenly, I became a scapegoat for our rare loss. "I can't believe you fouled that girl," Chelsea said. Other girls lit into me about missing shots.

"Like you didn't miss any?" I said. "We all could've done better." The argument stopped when our coaches entered the locker room, but I let the girls' words fester on the drive home. I cried myself to sleep that night and refused to attend practice the next day. The ill feelings didn't resolve until one of our coaches called a team meeting that evening to settle the matter. The girls apologized, I returned to practice, and no one mentioned the incident again.

It was a given that Chelsea became Sara's friend.

• • •

Every summer since second grade, Dawn and I had spent our weekends sleeping over at each other's houses, staying awake until daybreak, annoying our parents with our giggling. Only weeks prior to starting junior high, we had a dance party in her room. Nothing seemed wrong until she switched lunch tables to sit with Sara, stopped returning my calls, and rolled her eyes when I tried to talk to her. I don't remember asking why. Her dirty looks convinced me she was unapproachable. And if she no longer wanted to be my friend, I wasn't going to try to be hers. I simply accepted our broken friendship and carried the hurt until it stopped hurting.

Upon entering junior high, I lost three other friends to Sara. At the time, I thought it was because our common interests had changed. They had all made the cheerleading team. Maybe that provided them an exit out of a friendship they no longer wanted. I never found out why they rejected me. I only confronted others to express anger, not hurt. Had I offended them? Were they turned off by my aggressive responses toward Sara? Did they fear my defensiveness? If I cut off the most popular girl, what safeguarded them from my rejection? Maybe they ditched me before I had a chance to ditch them. Or maybe Sara had more to offer, like an older boyfriend and recognition amongst high schoolers. The loss of friendships not only weakened my social foundation, it also prevented my ex-friends from being targeted, increased their appeal, and secured their belonging. Together, none of them needed to take sole blame for their passive-aggression.[5]

Thankfully, I still had friends. I was just trying to figure out who they were to me and who I was to them. After Dawn dumped both Annie and me, we decided Bailey made us laugh, and Rylan didn't seem tied down to any other friends. Annie and I asked them if they wanted to hang out more. Just like that, we became a group and spent time with each other every weekend.

All of us had other friendships. Rylan and Annie played in the marching band, and Bailey captained the volleyball team, but our commonalities outweighed our differences. Boys didn't come between us. No power struggle existed amongst us. And, deep down, none of us were girly girls. Rylan chewed her nails more than I did, to the point they bled. I think that's one way she made herself tough. Bailey's curly hair was wild, a reflection of how much she cared about what others thought of her. And although many classmates considered Annie a shrinking violet, I knew she took time to develop her convictions in quiet. She always seemed in control of her emotions—one reason she was such a good friend for me.

The four of us shared that unspeakable spark that felt like we had been best friends forever. It strengthened every time we belly laughed about belting out the wrong song lyrics, and every time we rolled our eyes over Sara and her friends.

When Sara bragged about being voted class favorite for our yearbook, I was glad to hear my friends were as annoyed by her as I was. Anytime a classmate's disapproval of Sara and her friends matched mine and my friends, our group grew. All it took was a raised eyebrow at someone's comment.

Sara's group formed similarly, as she assumed the role of Queen Bee, and her friends became her Honeybees. I call them the Bees. These girls weren't the same kind of mean girls from the big screen, though. They didn't strut through the hallways in synchronous slow motion with their hair blowing in a breeze. They didn't accessorize popped-collar crop tops with designer handbags. People didn't run into locker doors or trip into garbage cans when they saw them. They came in all shapes and sizes, wore camouflage to hand-me-downs, and participated in everything from choir to Future Farmers of America. They had many friends, and few classmates challenged their authority.[6] If anyone did, the girls got them in trouble or recruited an older brother or sister to intimidate them. Most of the girls had older siblings, an advantage that not only provided protection but popularity as we moved into high school.

In late eighth grade, rumors about freshmen initiation circulated. Kevin worried about seniors turning him upside down in the toilet. He assured me upperclassmen didn't give girls swirlies, but I needed a strategy to avoid having my books knocked out of my hands.

Basketball provided me with self-esteem and recognition, but in high school I couldn't act as the same tough girl when I stepped off the court, or I'd literally get knocked down for it. So, I left my intensity in the gym and tucked away my stand-up-and-fight voice to follow the rules of a good girl.

I wrote friends encouraging notes and called people I wanted to get to know better. In the classroom, I earned good grades but didn't raise my hand to avoid coming off as a know-it-all. I smiled until my cheeks quivered. At lunch I made the rounds, recognizing people no matter their clique by saying hello and addressing them by name. I talked sweetly to boys. I switched from oversized sweaters to form-fitting T-shirts, curled my hair, wore mascara, and tanned. Passiveness mixed with just the right amount of confidence caused people to say, "She's so nice." Like basketball, it felt more productive to lift others up and invite them along the way instead of tearing others apart to clear the way. By acting kindly, getting along with almost everyone, and exhibiting the feminine image my classmates expected, I influenced what they thought of me. When I gave love, I fortified my fortress of friendship, which protected me before I became a vulnerable freshman.

• • •

I first learned that likability is measurable from Sara, when in middle school she told me her dream of becoming homecoming queen. The competition, left in the hands of our student body, recognized our school's favorite girls. Every fall and winter, each class chose one girl as its attendant, and the entire student body elected three senior girls. The senior with the most votes claimed queen. There were no binding requirements besides a mediocre grade point average, and only seniors could be voted to court twice. The homecoming queen didn't contribute to much of anything. She didn't adopt a service platform or organize any student activity. She didn't deliver a speech at graduation or return to crown next year's queen. Her biggest role was to stand in front of people for a weekend and look pretty wearing a tiara.

Sara said whoever won freshman homecoming attendant determined who would become queen as a senior. Undoubtedly, the title belonged to her. But the summer before high school, a shift occurred, and that fall, our classmates elected me freshman attendant. I officially offered my school more than wins on the basketball court. With my popularity increasing and Sara's decreasing, she and her friends embarked on a mission to regain their reign.[7]

The day of the announcement, someone told me Sara had accused me of spreading rumors about her and her boyfriend, Kent.

Just because I played Good Girl didn't mean True Me never emerged. I was still direct, but instead of blowing up in front of everyone, like I used to at the lunch table, I approached Sara alone in the hallway, a technique Dad taught me after learning conflict resolution at his job. "Why are you telling people I'm spreading rumors?"

"I'm not," she said.

"Who is? Why can't you and your friends just leave me alone?" I stormed away before she had a chance to respond.

Several class periods later, Kent hung over the railing as I descended the stairs. "Mind your own business and leave Sara alone," he said. He launched his gum at me and scurried away at the bell. He would be back, though, keen on hitting his target.

Only days later, at the county fair, my mom and her friend walked near the agricultural barns when a pick-up truck drove up from behind so closely that it nudged them off the path. "Watch where you're going!" they said, throwing their hands up as Kent drove by with Sara riding shotgun.

When our family returned home that evening, we listened to a message on our answering machine from Sheriff Deputy Conrad, who said Sara's parents filed a complaint against Mom for harassing Sara. They wanted Mom to leave their daughter alone. Deputy Conrad left no further instruction.

"Leave *her* alone?" Mom said, throwing her hands up again. "I'm the one who about got ran over!"

It seemed unnecessary to involve law enforcement, so Dad called Sara's father to figure out what was going on. By the way my dad paced, I could tell the conversation set him off. "This is crazy," Dad said. "We'll counteract if you try to uphold this."

As I eavesdropped, I blamed myself and wondered why I ever became friends with Sara. After the phone call, my parents instructed me to stay away from the Bees, and the drama soon died down.

Six months later, my parents befriended our new neighbors, the Smiths. Mr. Smith worked as a sheriff deputy. Eventually, my parents mentioned Deputy Conrad's message.

"Conrad? I know him," said Mr. Smith. "Why? What's he up to now?"

Standard protocol required Deputy Conrad to bring documentation of the grievance to our home. Mr. Smith checked into the matter and confirmed that no one had filed a complaint.

Although we never learned how the message came about, it's understandable how easily adults became involved. Sara's parents wanted happiness and success for her, as did mine for me. Naturally, our parents adopted the same negative feelings Sara and I experienced toward each other. It was our parents' instinct to protect us, albeit through different messages and resources, and their sentiments extended to our families' social spheres.

• • •

Not only did Sara and I learn opposite communication styles, we also competed differently. I always wanted to beat my opponents, but demoralizing Sara or any other girl didn't make sense to me. I liked winning because I wanted recognition for my individuality. Winning highlighted my capabilities and proved I could excel beyond limitations I placed on myself and others placed on me. My challenge was to not get sucked into the comparison trap. Maybe our health teacher, who measured our body fat percentage in front of our class and wrote our results on the board, thought confident girls helped support his lesson. It only further pitted us against each other, as did teachers who favored one of us over the other, boys who compared our physical features, and peers who played sides. As much as I fought to separate myself by participating in activities that Sara did not, we constantly competed for the admiration of our peers. And Sara and her friends always reminded me that I'd pay the consequences for winning.

A year later, after Sara won homecoming attendant, the Bee swarm intensified. They upped their dirty looks, called me names like "stuck-up," "goodie-goodie," and "rich snob," and told people I badmouthed them. When my name made announcements, they said I didn't deserve recognition. When I won awards, they said, "It's not fair." When my action-shots made the front page of the sports section, they mocked my expressions. "Why does she always need to smile and say hi to everyone?" Chelsea said. When I wore a dress, they told schoolmates, "She looks like a twelve-year-old." When I didn't wear makeup, they told me, "You look sick." One of them nicknamed my ponytail the horse's tail. "It's a compliment," she said, but it never felt like one. Tearing me down not only bonded them closer, but it more deeply united me and my friends and divided our two groups.

When I asked why the girls seemed to pick on me more than any other girl, friends, family, principals, and counselors said, "They're jealous." Jealousy. The classic reason why girls don't like each other and a supposed compliment to have other girls feel less valuable in comparison. I'm sure Sara heard the same thing. No one seemed to understand conflict between girls any other way. "Don't stoop to their level," people said. "Be the bigger person. Walk away. You'll end up stronger."

I still wonder why the girls did these kinds of things. Did creating drama make them feel important? Did they act this way because they struggled with their body image and confidence? When they overheard someone compliment me, did they feel like it took something away from them? Whatever the reasons, I wish I could've convinced those girls that God loves us all, and when we are secure in Him, we don't need to act mean toward others. But I was still figuring that out for myself.

My instincts told me to go off. Instead, I took the advice of friends and family to ignore the Bees. So, I rolled my eyes and pretended their behavior didn't bother me. This new approach required the same kind of mental toughness I used in basketball. Like ignoring smack-talk at the foul line, I learned to keep my mouth shut and beat them with my actions. I strived to pay more attention to my own game than the tactics they used to bring me down. Applying these same principles with the Bees helped defuse situations that would've otherwise become major problems. Even so, every time I suppressed my emotions, I stewed.

Basketball helped me counteract the Bees' negativity,

especially during junior year, when our team became the first girls' team in school history to earn a trip to the state tournament. That season, game nights shut down towns and filled our gym beyond maximum capacity. Our school held pep rallies, the local newspaper wrote feature stories about us, and businesses dressed marquees with messages of encouragement. Kids wrote to us to tell us they wanted to play basketball just like us. Friends decorated car windows and flew our school flag from the beds of their trucks.

Our team became closer than ever, and I developed a better friendship with Janeen, whom I had played with longer than any of the other girls. Off the court, we ran around town. Before games, we went on fast-food runs. I still have no idea how we played with supersized combo meals sloshing in our bellies. And although Coach never proved we toilet-papered his house, we knew he knew it was us, and we covered our mouths to hide our laughs after he confronted us. I wished Janeen and I had been closer sooner, because she turned out to be a solid friend.

The morning of our state tournament game, we loaded onto a charter bus to the cheers of our student body. Police escorted us to the arena, and school dismissed early. We fell two games short of the championship. Even so, we made our community so proud it continues to celebrate our team to this day. After our trip to state, I believed I could accomplish anything. I could never disappoint adoring fans. I had not yet learned that when you reach the top, some people keep chiseling until your foundation crumbles.

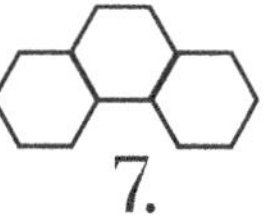

7.
DELEGATING DIRTY WORK

MOM GLOWED AS WE STOOD in front of a department store rack. Pink wasn't my favorite color. I tried guiding her to other options, but as I watched her stroke the satin, I softened, remembering she had hand-sewn her prom dress because her family couldn't afford to buy one. I thought of her when she was my age, scouring her house for coins to buy fuel when the gas man stopped coming and sharing a box of Rice Crispies with her dog when it was the only food in the cupboard. I headed to the dressing room, knowing I'd wear that dress to represent my mom's dream to provide more for her children.

On the day of the dance, I created a curly up-do and applied more makeup than usual. I had never worked so hard on my appearance. Outside the cafeteria, I stalled to fan my armpits. If I opened the door to drooping decorations, the dance would flop and fingers would point at me, leader of the prom committee. But the compliments of seniors carried me to the center of the empty dance floor, where fifteen of my friends and I showcased our disco-hip-hop-hoedown moves. We invited others to join, and our laughter grew. I envisioned that evening becoming a warm scrapbook memory until Melissa told me to turn around. Sara's friend, Zack, motioned me toward him.

Although Sara worked hard to get ahead of me, it seemed like she was always right behind me. In lines and at assemblies her voice stalked me, making it known she dominated our peers' attention. Even in our group yearbook pictures, out of all that space on the bleachers, she often sat close enough to touch me. Her presence served as a reminder that she wasn't going away, and I couldn't ignore her.

But ever since Sara won homecoming attendant, she seemed to slip farther into the background as her best friends stepped up to complete the group's dirty work. At prom, I turned to see Sara's Bees, Amber, Dawn, and Chelsea, laughing, pointing, and mocking my dance moves. Sara and Kent stood behind them, laughing.

"They said you look like shit. Your hair's dumb, and your dress is ugly," Zack said. Zack and Sara had known each other since elementary school. He was more of her friend than mine and hung out with the popular guys, who teased him because of his lisp. If those boys had made fun of me like that, I would've punched them. But Zack turned the attacks into jokes by acting like a drunk or cartoon characters, which secured his position as funnyman number two in our class. I assumed the teasing didn't bother him. Now I don't know how it couldn't, and I wonder if his jokes covered up his hurt feelings. If he understood how words wounded, why did he deliver such a harsh message to me? Did it help him feel important? Perhaps he was eager to displace negative attention onto someone else. Maybe it was easy for that someone else to be me because I never defended him.

Standing before him at prom, my smile dropped to my glittery, four-inch heels. How did they know where to jab deepest? "Stop!" I yelled to the girls. "Get a life." I threw them the double finger and nervously fell into rhythm with the chicken dance. I ignored them the rest of the night, until the lights turned on and Amber blocked my pathway to the door.

"We weren't talking about you," she said as she ran her shoulder into mine.

"What's your problem?" I said, but she kept walking.

Kevin, Annie, Amber's date, and a chaperone stared, speechless. Perhaps they wondered if I'd revert to middle-school me. Instead, I exited like a good girl and headed home to meet twenty of my friends for snacks and a movie.

I expected the Bees to retaliate as they always did, but none of them had ever come at me physically. Leave it to Amber. Within days of her moving to our school in eighth grade, she established herself as one of the most vocal girls in our class. She routinely gossiped about me to me in front of our math class with comments like, "I heard you hate Sara," or "Chelsea said you've been running your mouth about Sara." Math never came easily to me, and Amber's disruptions required me to stay after or use my lunch period to get extra help.

In high school, Amber didn't earn honor roll, play sports, or join many clubs. Mostly, she relied on friendships to fit in. Backing Sara no matter what and serving in this physically aggressive role provided Amber more inclusion than anything school had to offer.

After I told my parents what happened at prom, they contacted one of my school's administrators, Mr. Littlefield. Although he never addressed the girls' behavior or disciplined Amber for shoulder-bumping me, despite a chaperone witnessing it, he seemed concerned. He advised us to document harassment on or off school property, taking an I'll-deal-with-it-later approach. His next chance arrived shortly.

Whenever I left Chemistry, Amber shoulder-bumped me without making eye contact or speaking a word. It didn't matter if I raced out the door or hung back to avoid her; she wouldn't leave me alone. Sometimes I adjusted my stance, so she only threw me off balance. Other times she forced me into the lockers. I clenched my teeth and walked away every time, denying my instinct to push her back. My parents always informed Mr. Littlefield, but he claimed he couldn't discipline Amber because he didn't have proof. "All we can do is document new incidents," he said.

• • •

Like most of my peers, I felt safe in my high school of six hundred. Virtually no student went unaccounted. Teachers were involved in students' activities and therefore supervised better. That's why I didn't understand why someone couldn't catch Amber in action. Mr. Littlefield knew when and where she shoulder bumped me. All he needed to do was watch. Evidently, this kind of behavior was acceptable, as long as no one got caught.

Immediately following one of her run-ins, I went to Mr. Littlefield's office. "I'm tired of her pushing me. With what just happened at Columbine—"

"Wait a minute," he said. "Has anyone threatened you with any type of weapon? No one has held a gun to your head, have they?"

"No."

"You have no reason to be scared, then," he said.

Before Amber's aggressiveness, I was never bothered by the occasional fistfight that broke out in the lunchroom, or by the shotguns some of the boys kept in their unlocked trucks. The Columbine High School shooting had shaken the nation, though, and now I questioned my safety.

I deflated. I didn't like being told how to feel. Why didn't Mr. Littlefield take me seriously? Maybe he thought because nothing too dangerous had ever happened at our school, nothing ever would. Perhaps, to him, I was an annoyance or a dramatic teenager with the least significant problems amongst his students. Or was he frustrated because he didn't know what to do about Amber? Maybe he was too busy. Perhaps he was part of the 25 percent of educators who "see nothing wrong with bullying or put downs and consequently intervene in only 4 percent of bullying incidents."[8] To him, maybe we were just "kids being kids," girls who needed to learn how to handle our conflict independently. He never provided a clear-cut stance. He simply heard out my parents every time they complained, and said, "Keep documenting. The more, the better." Perhaps he more easily managed one upset family than multiple sets of hot Honeybee parents, most of whom were alumni and whose influence could negatively impact his public approval. Eventually, I understood the difficulty of disciplining for gossip and other secretive behaviors, but I never figured out why Mr. Littlefield downplayed my concerns and refused to stop Amber's shoulder bumps. I couldn't turn to him for help again.

My parents did their best with what they knew. They advised me to avoid Amber, but in a small town, ignoring an enemy isn't possible.

• • •

One weekend, as Rylan, Annie, Bailey, and I left Target, Amber and Chelsea entered. They whispered and giggled as they locked in on me. My friends and I shuffled into a cluster as the exit narrowed. That's what makes best friends, best friends. When pressure approaches, you walk through tight places together. No one could separate that kind of friendship—at least, that's what I thought as we braced ourselves for a Bee sting.

Bent on plowing into me, Amber penetrated our fortress. She and Chelsea kept walking. They fell into each other, laughing.

"Real nice," Annie said. "Classy move."

"Next time you run into me, you're gonna be sorry," I said. Bailey grabbed my arm and tugged me out the door.

"It's not worth it," she said.

"I want to rip her face off," Rylan growled over her shoulder.

We dove into Bailey's Ford Taurus, slammed the doors, and screamed in unison. A passerby stopped and cocked his head.

Bailey lowered her window. "We're all right. Nothin' to see here," she said as she cut her wheel hard and hit the gas.

When I got home, I blasted through the door. Mom and Dad were relaxing, watching television. "Next time she pushes me, I'm gonna knock her out," I said to my parents. "I'm sick of ignoring her. It doesn't work. Someone needs to put her in her—"

"Settle down," they said. "Let us handle this."

They contacted the sheriff's office, filed a complaint, and threatened to press charges. Before proceeding, they tried communicating with Amber's parents. However, law enforcement couldn't locate them. Her caretakers refused to talk.

I didn't know Amber came from a broken home. Perhaps what happened in her life affected her decision-making more than anyone would ever know. My parents did their best to help me understand why she targeted me. Maybe she wanted the happiness I had for herself. Parents who attended every ballgame. A dad who provided security. A mom who left notes in her packed lunches. A little sister who stole sweaters. A home she never had to box up and leave. Perhaps Amber felt marginalized, but amongst the Bees she fit in, elevating herself amongst them by fulfilling a role no one else would.[9]

8.
SUCKER PUNCHED

A FRIEND'S DAD HANDED my dad the flyer. "I thought you might want to know about this," he said. "Someone tacked it to our barn." Another copy was left in Bailey's car. Under an enlarged image of my yearbook headshot were the words *Hocking Ridge High School's Nark.*

"What's a nark?" I asked.

When I was four, I tasted beer and spit it out. I promised never to smoke a cigarette after lung cancer took both my grandparents within six months of each other. And the only parties I attended were the kind where kids got cranked up on Mountain Dew. I wasn't a tattletale, but because the Bees had labeled me a "goodie-goodie," my clean reputation was a convenient target.

My parents contacted the sheriff's department, and a detective came to our house. "Fingerprints are too hard to pick up off paper," he said. "I don't think this is anything to worry about. Just teenage mischief. It'll blow over soon." My parents then contacted an attorney, who agreed. No one seemed to be taking the shots at me seriously. I needed a break. Perhaps my enemies' fixation would fade with a summer of suntans, jobs, and family vacations.

But alongside these kinds of distractions also came less structure and enough boredom to keep my antagonists interested in me.

One afternoon, I turned on the computer and noticed an e-greeting from an unknown address, noneyodamnbidniz@----you.com, sent by Eric Foreman and Brad Ausmus. I didn't know them, but their names seemed familiar. Curious, I opened the "Parents' Day" card titled "a Father's Day poem that's MY dad." Its message: "Watch yo' back." Something told me this wasn't junk mail. My breath shortened, my fingertips shook, and my belly knotted. I yelled for Mom, who paused her yard work to come read the email. "What is this?" she said. She took screen shots. When Dad returned home from work, Mom explained what happened. "Do you think we're overreacting?" she said.

"I don't know, but let's find out," Dad said.

They agreed that because the email was a Parents' Day card, the message was meant for them as much as it was for me. All of us were sure Amber sent it, but we needed proof.

My parents contacted the sheriff's department and spoke with an investigator who provided instructions on how to trace the email. Locating online bullies did not require a court order then. First, my parents contacted the website and got the sender's internet service provider, which in turn provided the sender's home address—that of our longtime family friends, the Dawsons.

As babies, their son, Tyler, and I shared a playpen at our parents' cookouts. When we were five, we attended different elementary schools, and our families fell out of touch but reunited when Tyler and I met up again in middle school. Since then, our friendship had seemed unwavering.

"Why would he do this?" I asked.

"I don't know," Dad said. "But we're leaving to find out."

Although Tyler and I never had problems, I should've known he would deceive me. In middle school his crush was Sara, and now, in high school, he dated Chelsea. I felt stupid, especially after I realized Eric Foreman was a fictional character on *That '70s Show*, and Brad Ausmus played professional baseball. I'm sure Tyler found humor in that.

Every school has a Tyler: the guy who eats lotion to see if it really tastes like cucumber melon, breaks silence with a fart, and writes the most random comments in peoples' yearbooks. Tyler wore clown wigs, oversized glasses, rain boots on sunny days, and old man clothes from the thrift store. At sporting events, he heckled the opponents for everything from their athletic ability to how much they sweated to their body type and sock length. He always found a way to get attention.

My classmates and I didn't make a big deal about Tyler's actions, even when he made fun of people or annoyed us. We merely attributed his acts to immaturity and pardoned him as everyone's entertainer. However, when I became one of his targets, it opened my eyes. Now, as I recall his behavior, I'm regretful of times I did not defend others.

The most memorable of his showcases was when he threw french fries at Winnie, a learning-disabled student who sat at the end of our table. He wasted a whole order flipping them at her face. She flinched every time and seemed upset. "It's fun, isn't it?" he said.

Winnie's cheeks lifted. "Oh, Tyler, yer so funny." She burst into giggles and rocked. His friends looked away, covering their mouths. I rolled my eyes to my girlfriends.

"Boys are so stupid," I said.

Why didn't I rip those fries out of his hand? Winnie was my friend. We had ridden the bus together since elementary school and talked on the phone twice a week. Why didn't I protect her? Maybe I didn't want her to know it wasn't a joke. I might as well have thrown food at her too.

Ignoring Tyler was easier than offending him and his friends. Coming against him could jeopardize my popularity. But now, as his target, I changed my stance.

After my parents explained to the Dawsons my trouble with the Bees, Mrs. Dawson said, "I wouldn't blame her if she knocked someone's lights out." Tyler admitted he and his best friend, Richard, also my friend, sent the message. He played it off as a joke until our parents told him the legal repercussions. My parents simply asked for apologies. The Dawsons said they were sorry, but Richard's mom refused because Richard denied involvement. For that, I instantly wrote him out of my life. Tyler headed to my house to apologize.

The sky rumbled. Lightning flashed above the skylights, and the tension rose inside me. I fell onto the couch, overcome by a downpour. *This is going to be awkward. What will we say? Should I tell him off? Is he really sorry? Maybe he just doesn't wanna go to juvie. Why do I have to do this? What did I ever do to him?*

Tyler walked to my door, chin to chest, stiff-armed and tight-fisted. "You . . . probably know . . . what I've come to talk about," he said.

I nodded my head and invited him in.

"Sorry," he said. "I never meant for any of this to be such a big deal."

I accepted his apology. "Why did you guys send it?"

He stared at the floor, shrugged, and held his hands out, the same way he acted when a teacher wanted to know who threw spit wads at the board.

"Come on, Tyler. Who are you covering for?"

"No one."

"Tyler."

Thunder cracked, and we both jumped.

"Chelsea and Amber. We didn't know what they meant by it, though."

Tyler knew the girls caused me trouble. Why did he allow them to influence him? Maybe he found himself in the same predicament I found myself in when he threw fries at Winnie.

The rain tapered. Hope peeked through a blanket of gray. "Tyler, you can't let those girls get to you. They don't like me, so they're gonna try to drag you into things."

"Yeah, I don't want anything like this to ever happen again," he said.

Our reconciliation ended more promisingly than any confrontation I had ever had. I believed we had mended our friendship.

9.
SYSTEM FAILURE

AS SUMMER FADED, I only heard about Tyler's social life and increasing loyalty to the Bees through other people. Perhaps he had only said he was sorry to appease our parents. Regardless, my disappointment lessened with the approach of senior year, that long-awaited year when I expected to create the most memorable moments of my life.

School started smoothly. The Bees had left me alone after the email. To help me avoid them, my guidance counselor, Mr. Brown, had changed four of my classes to study halls (although the limit was two). And Chelsea had decided not to play basketball. I was sure this was the year I'd have fewer problems, but I had forgotten how problematic homecoming could be.

Our student body would vote for three senior girls. Whoever earned the most votes would be queen. Elections took place on a Friday morning. In first-period study hall, my chest became heavy as the teacher distributed the ballots. This is it—the whole school's final say about which girl they treasured most.

After five minutes, the teacher collected the votes, and a group of guy friends gave me fist-pumps. The bell rang, and I walked through the hallways, where students told me they had circled my name. Underclassmen girls tugged my shirt sleeves. "You're definitely gonna win," a freshman said.

Throughout the day, more students told me the same. I enjoyed their compliments and smiled my thank-yous, careful not to show too much excitement. The competitor inside me wanted to burst into a victory jump, but even when I knew my basketball team was going to win, I never celebrated until the buzzer sounded. It wasn't good sportsmanship. Neither could I celebrate the same way I did on the court. It wasn't proper for nice girls to recognize popularity, and if curtsying like a lady was what it took to win, that's the game I would play.[10]

The following Monday, I found out my classmates selected me as a queen candidate along with Sara and one of her Bees. The homecoming advisor, Mrs. Norris, and Mr. Littlefield knew the results, but they wouldn't announce the winner until the pep rally in two weeks. I expected a disapproving buzz, but the day was strangely quiet, like the time I waded under our pool slide, seeking shelter from the sun, and was dive-bombed by wasps. Weeks later I still felt as if I had just been stung. For years, every time a wasp buzzed near me, the sound reminded me of the pain they caused. Chills radiated across my skin, and I would take off running until I was sure I was out of their territory.

The day of the announcement, I stayed after school for the volleyball games, to take photos for the yearbook. While the junior varsity team warmed up, several varsity players urgently approached me. Minutes before, at the water fountain, Tyler told them and anyone else who would listen how I had ruined his previous weekend.

"Huh?" So far this school year, Tyler and I had said hello in the hallways twice.

"He said you snitched on Amber's party to the police," said a team captain. "Now they're in trouble. You got Sara kicked off homecoming court. How could you do that?"

"I didn't tell on them. I didn't even know about their stupid party," I said.

Eventually, I learned what had happened through a public incident report. Amber's next-door neighbor called the sheriff to report her noisy party. Amber was arrested on several counts: resisting arrest, obstructing official business, and underage consumption of alcohol. Sara, Dawn, and five Bees weren't arrested but were reportedly suspected of underage drinking. Standard procedure required the sheriff to notify the school of the students' activities.

Earlier in the day, Sara and several football players were suspended for two games for breaking their athletic drug and alcohol contracts. A panel of faculty decided Sara could resign from homecoming court or they would vote to determine whether she should remain or be kicked off. Sara refused to step down, so the panel voted her off. The senior girl who had been in fourth place filled the opening.

"I didn't do any of that," I said. "He's lying." My defense didn't matter. The whole volleyball team seemed convinced. Players approached me and said, "I heard you got Sara thrown off court." Others, curious as to why I appeared upset, joined the huddle to listen. Soon, the entire school would believe the news.

Although Sara and her friends were nowhere near, I felt eleven years old again. The same tactics used on our middle-school playground had become more sophisticated. Sara and her friends needed to relocate the negative attention surrounding them. Who else would make such an easy target to transfer blame onto?

If only I would've stepped away to consider how the story changed by the time it made its way to me. If only I had a team to pull me into a huddle like in biddy ball and remind me to play like I practiced, or an administrator who took me seriously, calmed me, and supported me with logical problem-solving. If only I had allowed the truth to play out, students would have forgotten about the rumor in a week. I could have saved myself stress. But my emotional adolescent brain couldn't separate fear from reality.[11] Gripped by the equally immature reactions of my peers, I only focused on how everyone seemed to believe Tyler.

I misunderstood that the rumor had less to do with me and everything to do with Tyler impressing the Bees and covering their mistakes. My throat swelled. My belly burned, and my cheeks flushed. I needed to stop him, to stop them. I faced two choices: accept mistreatment or protect my reputation. Everyone already thought I hated Sara and her friends. What did I have to lose if I stood up to one of them, once and for all?

More than I ever realized.

I searched for Tyler, letting everyone I passed know I was going to put him in his place. I found him near the gym, playing hacky sack with friends.

"Can I talk to you outside?"

I walked ahead to make sure no one was around and assumed my hands-on-hips-head-bobbin'-give-me-an-explanation-now stance. "What did I ever do to you? Why are you spreading rumors about me? Why do you keep doing this?"

His eyes lowered. "I didn't say anything," he said. "I don't know why you're so mad."

"You can't even look at me. I know you're lying."

He raised his gaze but couldn't resist the same grin he expressed whenever he got in trouble because of his jokes. I hated that smirk, so I tried to knock it off his face.

His mouth opened. His forehead frowned, and his eyes widened. He touched his cheekbone. I threw a second punch, sure I could knock away his smugness and prevent the rest of them from saying anything mean about me ever again.

"You hit me. I can't believe you just hit me." He scurried into the gym, and I stomped toward the opposite entrance, where one of my basketball coaches met me.

"What did you do?" he said.

"He deserved it."

I wasn't about to plead for understanding. No grown-ups seemed to understand except my parents. I rushed out of the gym and called home. Mom instructed me to stay away from Tyler and the Bees and to stay put. When she arrived, she listened to me ramble. Leaning into a wall, she sighed, likely envisioning the impending issues I never considered.

That night, our friendship with the Dawsons ended. Once, Mrs. Dawson had said she wouldn't blame me if I were to knock someone's lights out. I guess she meant anyone but her child. Unlike before, they declined to analyze their son's contribution to our new problem. Instead, they threatened to file a complaint with the sheriff, and I cried myself to sleep.

The next morning, the school secretary summoned me to the office. "Do you know why I called you here?" Mr. Littlefield said. "Tyler's mom just left. She's angry. Another parent saw you punch him."

"So?" I said. "It was after school hours."

"Doesn't matter. You were on school property," he said. "It wasn't the right thing to do. You made a bad decision. A mistake you have to learn from."

Bad decision? At least I know how to make a decision.

I had stood up against dishonesty and fought for what I believed was right. Why was it such a big deal all of the sudden? I had never seen a boy who cried about a girl picking on him receive much empathy from adults. On my elementary school playground it was acceptable, even commendable, to punch boys who picked on me. I got away with it when one chased me around our town's festival, spraying silly string in my hair until it matted. I warned him repeatedly, but he kept spraying until I gave him my right hook. I never got in trouble, and he never bothered me again.

In seventh grade while standing in line to leave class, a boy grabbed my butt. I jerked around with my fist up, demanding to know who did it. When our teacher interrupted to find out what happened, she looked at the boys and said, "I wouldn't blame her if she punched one of you." When the bell rang, we flooded into the hallway, where I assured the boys that if I found out who did it, I would deck him. Why not? I had the teacher's blessing.

I never got into too much trouble. Once, in kindergarten, I sat in timeout, my punishment for leaving my classroom. In second grade, I acted as an accomplice to a party that peeked in our "What's it?" box, a guessing game we played with our teacher. For that, we stood along the fence for three recesses. In junior high, I received two demerits when I didn't change clothes for gym class. I ended up in the principal's office for kissing my boyfriend. And my basketball coach made me apologize for back talking an assistant coach. I tested boundaries and learned to recognize my disobedience, but I never considered how to react when the rules failed me.

"You have a five-day out-of-school suspension," Mr. Littlefield said as he tilted in his squeaky 1970s polyester roller chair. I silently smoldered, wishing he would tip over. I wondered, why could the Bees bully me without repercussion, and I just had to take it? Were bad decisions acceptable as long as no one got caught? The lost-cause boys usually only received in-school suspensions for fighting. Even my dad had only received a three-day suspension when he coldcocked a boy who harassed him with one too many love letters.

For six months, my dad dealt with the boy's harassing phone calls and letters with naked pictures of himself sent through the mail or slipped into my dad's locker. After an English teacher matched the handwriting in a letter to one of her students, the principal promised to handle the matter, but he never did. Dad finally got fed up and landed one punch in stride that knocked the boy unconscious. The principal got so angry at my dad for handling the matter, he seized my dad by the throat until he blacked out.

I never knew about that story until I was an adult, but now I see how it mirrored mine, and I wonder if Mr. Littlefield saw the similarity before I could. He had started his teaching career around the same time my dad was in high school. Did Dad's action leave such an impression on him that it factored into my punishment twenty-five years later? He couldn't strangle me, but he could send a most disapproving message. A five-day out-of-school suspension was the maximum punishment before expulsion.

Looking back, I understand why Mr. Littlefield suspended me. I hurt Tyler. I violated the serious misconduct code. I deserved to be disciplined. Mr. Littlefield was simply doing his job. Although I still wonder if my steep punishment was meant not only to send a message to me but also as a way to make my dad continue to pay for his past.

What I didn't understand was why Mr. Littlefield didn't implement the psychological harassment/menacing code to punish anyone else. (At the time, no anti-bullying rules existed in our student handbook.) What was the difference between a black eye and a black mark? Throwing two punches felt like justification for his lack of enforcement. But my feelings didn't matter, only my actions. Mr. Littlefield never punished anyone else. Nor did he question why I had punched Tyler. I was the person most sensitive to our school's inability to deal with bullying. With me to blame, the previous problems could be displaced or concealed, and the system could resist change.[12]

I spent the rest of the week at home. Faculty voted for me to remain on the homecoming court, a decision that angered Sara and her family, understandably. It was unfair. We both made mistakes and broke policies, and we were both punished accordingly. No written rule supported how either of our mistakes affected us on the homecoming court. The panel should have removed both of us or neither of us. Why not simply leave things as they were instead of fostering animosity between two girls, their friends, and their families? I don't know why the panel voted to keep me and not Sara. I don't believe they liked me better, although I heard it might have been because they didn't like Tyler.

Once the Bees found out I was still on the court, they shifted the controversy from Tyler's black eye to the wrong they believed I had done to Sara. "The only reason she punched Tyler was to make sure she won homecoming queen and Sara didn't," Chelsea said.

On the contrary, hitting Tyler was never about winning. It was about losing friendship, respect, resources, and my sense of reality. Whether or not our peers believed the girls, many students sensed the realignment of power and joined the Bees. The response of the student body crushed me more than any punishment from the rulebook. Few peers gave the same kind of consideration to Sara's mistake because mine overshadowed it. Partying was more easily forgiven than an attack against two beloved central figures.

The week of my suspension, Melissa called to inform me of my peers' responses. As a freshman, Melissa had renounced her allegiance to the Bees, and we became steady friends. I don't know of any defining moment that shifted our relationship. She just suddenly became one of those girls with whom I laughed for no reason. All it took was one look and we could no longer contain ourselves. We caused such a ruckus one day that our teacher made us move our desks into the hallway, which we preferred over her class.

Despite all of our laughing, there was always something about Melissa that made me suspicious. Maybe it was how she used to bounce between my friends and Sara's on the playground, the deliverer of our she-said-they-said remarks. I couldn't prove she had ever done anything to me. Maybe I was paranoid because I never apologized for excluding her from the oak tree. I was just relieved she hadn't held it against me and felt I owed it to her to trust her until I had a reason not to.

Only weeks before my suspension, my classmates had voted me "Best Personality" in the senior class. Now, according to Melissa, they called me "Rich Bitch."

"Who's calling me that?" I said, floored to learn that friends from every social circle had turned against me. Melissa assured me that she stood up for me, but it hardly buffered my hurt.

Out of all the names, why that? Why bring my parents' finances into this? Money had nothing to do with my acting out. Rather, the name seemed to reveal what they really thought about not only me but my family. I had learned not to talk about my parents' income at school or with friends, but that didn't protect me from harsh words. On the inside, the attack lit up my resolve to defend my family. I immediately wrote off each name-caller and vowed never to speak to them again. Outwardly, my only responses to Melissa were, "What did I ever do to them?" and, "Thanks for sticking up for me." I hung up and threw my phone.

That week Melissa called me every day after school. As much as I appreciated her loyalty, I wondered why she seemed so eager to present bad news to me. I couldn't take hearing much more. I let her third call go to voicemail. Kevin and Bailey didn't tell me every detail like Melissa, but they confirmed what she said and filled me in on which people I could trust.

Although I still had many friends who supported me, at the time it seemed like the whole school had turned against me.

Parents, my graduated teammates, and customers at the butcher shop expressed opinions. It seemed like everyone was eager to say something. Few knew I was bullied; therefore, many were dumbstruck by my striking out.[13] The only way it made sense to some people was to attribute it to my dad's past behaviors. "The apple doesn't fall far from the tree," they said.

During lunch Zack circulated a notebook petition to have me disqualified from homecoming court and recruited others to throw food at me while I rode in the parade. Kevin, Johnny, and Ethan stood up to him. Kevin told me Ethan said, "We aren't doing that. Tami's our friend." Ethan and I had figured out how to remain friends after our break-up. I wondered if he finally recognized Chelsea's tactics and felt that he owed it to me to stand up. I appreciated his friendship and believed I could count on him this time.

So many students threatened to vandalize my house that my parents set up a surveillance camera, which caught Tyler and Richard in our driveway one night. Dad chased them away before they did any damage, aware that it wouldn't do any good to tell their parents.

The following week when I returned to school, I braced myself. I wished for their reactions to only be hearsay, but I immediately saw people ignore me or cast mean looks. Just before the first-period bell rang, a classmate screamed at me. "Getting Sara kicked off court was something you had no right to do!" she said. "I hope you get everything you have comin' to you!" The hallway had emptied except for my guidance counselor, Mr. Brown, who stared and then walked away as if to say, "You're on your own, kid." I froze. If this was how my day started, I wasn't sure if I should face the rest of it or run.

Within a few days, a handful of people had invoked uproar in an entire community, and I played right into it. I can only imagine how helpless my parents felt as I retreated to my bedroom every afternoon. They had tried to prevent this. They saw me pushed to my limit and couldn't provide a solution. All they could do was protect me the best they knew how. They took their concerns to Mr. Littlefield. If my classmates had elected me queen, my parents wanted to plan for my safety. Mr. Littlefield refused to reveal the winner, though, and instead called for a re-vote. "If we leave things like they are, it could make everything worse," he said. Maybe he was right, or maybe it would've finally extinguished the fire. All I knew then was that his decision felt like the times on the playground when Sara changed the rules mid-game. I wanted to quit, but my parents said, "You quit—they win."

For the longest time, I didn't understand that a do-over appeased a public that would never reward a rule breaker. Or that it safeguarded Mr. Littlefield from disapproving parents and peers. I just knew I had to remain on the court, even if it meant feeling double-crossed by the people who put me there.

10.
DEAD GIRL WALKING

A WEEK LATER, the dreaded day of the crowning captured me. First, I needed to survive the pep rally. I lurched toward the warm gym, preparing to face hundreds of booing students who planned to throw food at me. Maybe if I had played princess more and in the dirt less, I would've worked harder to avoid a moment like this.

The other attendants, with two escorts each, gathered in a hallway. Two weeks earlier, my friends told me that one of mine, Blaine, wanted me to be his girlfriend, but since I punched Tyler, Blaine treated me as if I didn't exist. As we waited, he laughed at the others' inside jokes. My only relief came when Kevin showed up. Kevin was my other escort, and I knew he would help me through this better than anyone.

As voices floated through the hallway, I clasped my hands to lessen my trembling. Every beat of the marching band's bass drums knocked my heart lower, until the screech of Mr. Littlefield's microphone sent it screaming into my throat.

"Representing the freshmen class," he said. "And the seniors . . ." Amidst my fantasies of worst-case scenarios, I closed my eyes, inhaled deeply, and squeezed Kevin's bicep, which squeezed back. The loudspeakers moaned my name. I prayed no one would throw anything or rush the court. In ways my entrance was better than I imagined. Hardly anyone booed, and I didn't get hit with tomatoes like some kids said I would. And, in other ways, it was as bad as I expected. Cheers erupted for Blaine as he rushed ahead of us with his hands in his pockets. I should've known he would do this.

Two months earlier, we had been roller skating when I fell. I landed on my wrist and broke my bracelet. Blaine laughed. The imprint of my bracelet stung. My blood surfaced. "Aren't you gonna help me up?" I yelled. Bailey and Rylan swooped in and pulled me up by my arms. I skated on with them, determined to hide my hurt. Right there, in the middle of that rink, I should've told him off. I should've ended what wasn't meant to be. Maybe I could've asked another boy who would've been brave enough to escort me onto that court. Instead, I had accepted that boys did dumb things, and now I paid for it.

Don't cry, I thought. Zack and several boys turned their backs. I clenched my teeth and forced a quarter smile, blurring the crowd into a tie-dyed mess, morphing the noise into a confusion of static pitches. I had been on that court before, tuning out opposing fans' rude comments. I knew how to work through that kind of pressure, but how was I supposed to withstand the disapproval of my home team?

I willed away my tears and focused on the top row, where the loners slouched. I envied them for seeming not to care. With folded arms and a cocked head, Laney Johnson chewed her gum like a cow chews cud. I wondered if she remembered why we were called to the principal's office in fifth grade and connected it to Chelsea yelling at me now. My downsized group of friends stood, arms crossed, on the bottom row. Other than Bailey and Rylan screaming once at the Bees, my friends stayed quiet. I longed for their help, but as badly as I wanted them to save me, and perhaps as much as they, too, wanted saved, I knew there wasn't anything anyone could do. Standing at mid-court, I laid to rest my popularity, confused as to why I had ever needed it.

Why had I spent so much time trying to get people to like me only to end up in a situation like this? Sometimes I had acted proper when all I wanted to do was yell at someone. I had dressed up to impress boys who now acted repulsed to see me dressed up. I felt as if I had gone out of my way to support people who never intended to do the same for me.

When I look at the photo that captured that scene, I see myself just trying to survive the moment. At the time, I couldn't summarize everything I was feeling, but now I realize I wasn't hurt over losing a title to the Bees. It wasn't even about earning my peers' approval. It was about keeping it. I was hurt because I had lost their love. I wanted it always and forever, but because high school has a way of branding us, I believed I didn't have another chance to redeem myself. I felt deceived. I ignored that thing Mom told me never to do—I hated. I not only hated so many of them for turning against me, I hated myself for caring so much. Had I known how that choice would grip my future, I would've resisted.

When Mr. Littlefield announced another candidate's name as the winner, the Bee colony erupted. They screamed their woo-hoos and pumped their fists, looking at me, laughing. Unsurprised yet mortified, I walked toward the queen.

What am I doing? I had no idea, but I had to do something. Whenever I lost a basketball game, I still shook hands with my opponents.

"Congratulations," I said as I hugged her. She stiffened. Others gasped.

"Hit 'er!" said a boy.

"Go back to yer place in line," someone said.

"Gimme a break!" said Chelsea.

I hated that I had hugged her. Was it right? Was it wrong? I didn't know, but it didn't feel like me. I wished I had extended a handshake instead. The bell rang. Some of the Bees mingled with their queen while the rest of the student body stormed the doors to the parking lot. Everyone seemed to separate school from wherever they were headed. After my ball games, people always waited to congratulate or console me, but I had never stood out on that court feeling more alone than I did now. Kevin, Melissa, and Melissa's best friend, Kara, were my only friends who stayed. "You okay?" Kevin said, assuring me that if I wasn't he would skip golf practice to take me home. Melissa and Kara offered hugs.

Melissa and Kara were more like see-you-at-school friends than sleepover friends. Out of all of my friends, I wasn't sure why they were the ones who stuck around. Maybe it proved Melissa really had forgiven me for the incident at the oak tree. Maybe Kara stayed only because she was always with Melissa. Or maybe she remembered me inviting her to my lunch table when she was new. In ninth grade, Kara had transferred from a private school. At first, I didn't see how she fit in with my friends and me. She sat straight and still, with her elbows off the lunch table. But her scrunched-nose giggle soon found its place amongst us. I was glad to see it hadn't left. "My feet feel like cinder blocks," I said. Melissa grabbed my shoulders and turned me toward a door. I appreciated the nudge.

Reluctantly, I walked to the cafeteria to fulfill my decorating duties, mostly to prove I hadn't gone home to throw a pity party. Mrs. Norris and two freshmen girls, giddy about glitter, didn't even notice me. *Why am I still here?* Because normally I followed the rules and fulfilled commitments. I let go of a balloon. It looped its way to the floor, reminding me of my reputation. *Screw this.*

I stomped to my car. Fury squashed my gas pedal, and tears blurred my windshield. I swerved into our driveway, skidded to a stop, and marched to my room to scream into my pillow.

My parents knew what happened.

"Please don't make me go tonight," I said.

"You're going," Mom said. "You got yourself into this mess. You're gonna have to walk through it."

A real rebel would've run away or taken gasoline and a lighter. I decided to wear tennis shoes with my dress, hoping to irk the old hens and roosters who thought it unladylike. Sure enough, as soon as I entered the gates of the stadium, one music booster mother said to another, "Can you believe she's wearing tennis shoes?" She was the same woman from church who sparked the chatter about Miss Sally being a witch. But before I could backtalk her, my attention shifted to five sparkling golf carts, which were to transport each attendant around the track. The cheerleaders, who were responsible for decorating the carts, left mine plain and muddy. Mom pulled a cornhusk from its wheel well, found a cloth, scrubbed the seat, and helped me hang my signs, all the while drawing a crowd of onlookers. I wanted to say, "Take a picture," but I held it in until my hands shook. The lack of help made me aware of the absence of my friends, some of whom hadn't yet arrived and others who protested by not coming.

Ten minutes before I walked across the field, Blaine stood me up. "He's not coming," Kevin said. I started to freak out.

"Calm down," Mom said.

"Who do you want me to go ask?" said Kevin.

"It's too late to find a replacement," Mrs. Norris said. "We can't change the program."

How could she not understand this had less to do with delivering a post-it note to the press box and everything to do with my humiliation? I was sure people would talk about why I only had one escort and that would attract more negative attention. I could feel their judgment heat up my neck. Kevin and Mom argued with Mrs. Norris while I wandered to my golf cart.

I sat there with my head lowered, wanting to hijack the cart so I could run over her. I imagined riding past the packed bleachers and flipping the finger to everyone. I could commando roll onto the second curve of the track, which would line up a straight path for me to sprint home. But the cart rolled forward, and I still cared too much about what everyone thought. Instead, I smiled and waved to show people they couldn't hurt me.

At the fifty-yard line, I sighed with relief when I saw Kevin with our friend Greg, who wore a button-down shirt and tie. He said he kept dress clothes in the trunk of his car for golf matches, but something told me he had prepared for this moment. I gripped their arms as the announcer read my bio.

"You're doin' great," the boys said.

As we walked past the woodwind section of the marching band, Annie and I exchanged glances. Her eyes said, "I'm here for you." Kevin must have felt me stall, looking for the comfort of one of Rylan's eye rolls. "Keep going. It's almost over," he said, just like he had during frozen push-ups in biddy ball.

In the background the announcer noted my awards—awards that felt like they meant nothing, just like the moment in which I now found myself. On the home sideline, under buzzing lights, I wanted that tiara more than ever—so I could snap it and stomp on it.

When the ceremony ended, I froze, feeling more exposed than ever because there was no next step. As the football team crowded me off the sideline, panic shot through me. I took off, losing Kevin on the stairs of the crowded bleachers. The court had already gathered together, huddled under blankets, blowing on hot chocolate. Even if I wanted to sit with them, I doubted they would make space. I couldn't seek comfort from Annie and Rylan because they couldn't leave the band. I had no idea where Bailey was. Someone called my name, but I couldn't search the bleachers, or I would see all of those eyes. On a direct path to my parents, I silently pleaded for them to take me home. They didn't want to be there any longer than I did, but we stayed for the slowest three quarters of football I've ever watched.

The next day, I attended the dance to fulfill the requirement of a group photograph and the court's procession onto the dance floor, where I believed barely supervised students would boo me.

But my friends' cheers deafened any heckles, bringing out my smile for the first time in weeks. Melissa and Kara screamed louder than I had ever heard them scream. Bailey danced in a circle like she was twirling a lasso above her head. And I heard Annie's soulful, unrestrained laugh. I stopped in front of Zack, whose hands were in his pockets, and bowed to my friends. I hoped it showed everyone I wasn't defeated. Surely, the worst was over.

11. NO GOING BACK

AFTER HOMECOMING WEEKEND I expected people to move on, but school staff members gossiped, and teachers condoned classroom slam sessions. When I entered one of those chaotic scenes, silence blanketed the room.

"What's everyone talking about?" I asked.

"Rreeear!" Zack screeched, clawing at the air.

Teachers hastily straightened their desks, hid behind newspapers, or promptly asked for homework. Newspaper clippings or pictures of me didn't hang on bulletin boards too long before being defaced, littered on the floors, and swept into a pile of trash, which I often beat the janitors to throwing away. Juvenile scribbling decorated my locker. And I cringed every time I entered the restroom, where someone had written *Tami is a bitch* on a stall door. I treated school like my parents treated their yellow legal pad. If I had a bad day, I'd crumple it up, throw it in my mental wastebasket, and look at the next day as a blank sheet. But the backlash became more difficult to face each day, and I was running out of paper.

At the end of my junior year, when Amber kept shoulder-bumping me, I considered homeschooling. The only thing

I knew about homeschooling was from the kids who gathered at the Holiness Church across the street from my elementary school. At recess they played volleyball, the girls wore head coverings and light-washed denim, and they left in a white Ford Econoline van. I had no idea how they did school, and I didn't really want to wear a head covering, but they proved there was an alternative. At that time, no online programs existed, so I asked Mr. Brown about my options.

"You've put in twelve years here," he said. "Don't you think it would be more satisfying to receive a diploma with our school's name on it?"

Maybe he bought into the stereotype that homeschooled kids are anti-social and illiterate. How could they possibly receive an adequate education if they didn't participate in our system? He never recommended another option, like the career center. Maybe he couldn't envision me as a cosmetologist, but he never even asked what I wanted to do beyond high school. Whatever his reason, I simply accepted his dismissal of my idea and wondered how I'd make it through six more months of school.

Although I hadn't been to church in six years, I still believed in God. I had started thinking about Him more after Dawn criticized me. In response to a Q&A in the sports section of the newspaper, I replied I'd give anything to meet God. "That's the stupidest thing I've ever read," she said to her math class. "No one even knows if God's real." In a faith-centered community, that kind of doubt seemed like something one should keep private. Most of the Bees attended church. So, I wasn't sure why she would say something that her own friends would disagree with. Now, I wonder if it was because she struggled with faith. Maybe

Dawn thought my statement was confident, but I had a lot of uncertainty to figure out.

Every night in bed I asked, "Why is this happening?" But I never heard an answer. God seemed so high in the sky that I wondered if He even heard me. When I think back, I realize He was there. When I cried myself to sleep, He sent sweet messages of comfort through my kitties, who kneaded the blanket over my belly, purred into my ear, and slept by my head. Or through Mom, peeking into my room to remind me to grab my jersey out of the dryer in the morning.

God was as close to me as I allowed, and I only allowed Him into a narrow window. I didn't talk to Him as I struggled throughout the day. I only took my concerns to Him at bedtime when I said the "Now I lay me down to sleep" prayer. I wanted Him to speak to me, but I didn't recognize that I had pushed Him aside because I sought the sound of others' approval more. How could I expect a revelation from God when I had spent the last six years quieting Him? No wonder I didn't recognize His gentle consolations. I was too consumed in my circumstances to hear anything other than the emotions swirling in my mind.

Every morning, I buried myself amongst my stuffed animals and held my breath, hoping to make Mom think I had already left. It never worked. To wake me, she shook my shoulders or pulled me out by my ankles, only stopping when I kicked her. Arising with a stiff neck and throbbing temples, I bypassed my toothbrush, makeup, and breakfast, and dragged out the door in my pajamas.

School shouldn't have felt that difficult. I didn't do much. Four study halls sounded good at the beginning of the year, but now I resented them. While the solution required me to withdraw from several electives, it felt unfair that none of the Bees had to rearrange their schedules. I really wanted to take drama, but it was known as a class that the popular kids took. And I still wish I had enrolled in shop class with Rylan. Any girl who can run a power saw earns points in my book, but I convinced her I didn't take it because I was scared I'd cut off a finger. Out of the few subjects I took, I couldn't entirely avoid the Bees or their loyalists.

As part of an English assignment, several boys, including Johnny, made a video using our biddy ball trophies to poke fun at my family. One boy boasted to a mutual family friend about how it would upset me, which is how we found out about it. Dad contacted Mr. Littlefield, who confiscated the video. He said it didn't contain anything offensive but wouldn't allow my parents to watch it.

"Change of plans," our teacher said. "A group of you made a video you'll need to redo. You know who you are and why we aren't watching it." From the back row of the classroom, I smirked as the boys' shoulders dropped.

Soon after, someone stole my English folder from the class file cabinet, which contained sketches and free writing—my creativity and my release. I don't know why anyone wanted it, other than to trash another piece of me. It felt like the best of what was inside of me wasn't worth anything to them, and they were trying to tell me it shouldn't mean anything to me either.

As for the rest of my classes, I stopped studying. I had already been accepted to a college, so I no longer cared about my grade point average. I whizzed through tests, filling in whatever bubbled letter caught my eye. Contrary to what I had heard, *C* was not the best guess, but at least I finished tests quickly so I could rest my head on my folded arms.

Gradually, clubs excluded me. I hoped they had become disorganized and no longer gathered, but when I eavesdropped on student council and National Honor Society meetings, I knew it was no mistake that I hadn't been included. A year later, my yearbook confirmed that someone filled my role as secretary of the student council. Bailey served as treasurer. Why hadn't she told me?

• • •

At least they couldn't replace me at basketball. My team needed my skills and leadership, and I needed them to get my mind off my problems, encourage others, and contribute to something greater. Ball was my therapy. It was where I established rhythm, where I got lost in the swoosh of the net and the squeak of my shoes as I ran patterns. And it was where I could count on certain people, like Janeen, to treat me like they always had.

Every year Janeen and I made sure our lockers were side by side. On bus rides, it was our ritual to sit across from each other. And we prayed together before every game. One of my greatest comforts that year was knowing that, no matter my mood, I could arrive in the locker room and Janeen remained the same. She wouldn't ask questions. She'd just grab my favorite ball and set it by my locker, and that meant *let's shoot*. But throughout the season, holes formed in my safety net.

Off the court, some of my teammates laughed at me and talked about me behind my back but within earshot. "She's a bossy bitch," a junior said. Several of them were rumored to have toilet-papered our pool fence and littered our yard with cheese puffs. In practice and in games I yelled, "I'm open. Pass the ball!" The girls ignored me.

Twice I left practice in the middle of drills, steps away from packing my locker, but I returned each time. I blamed our coach, who failed to correct my teammates' behaviors or nurture our cohesion. When I tried to talk to him about it, he said, "We don't need any problems going into the state tournament."

Throughout my basketball career, whether I played on a winning or losing team, I mostly had healthy relationships with my teammates. When we experienced issues we found ways, either on our own or through our coaches' discipline, to make amends and progress. Now I worked with people I didn't get along with and who didn't seem to share the same goals. It was too late in the season to transfer to another school, so I kept playing, fearful my college coaches wouldn't approve of me quitting.

My teammates weren't the only ones who made basketball uncomfortable. During games, boys and one of my former teammates, Gracie, booed me. "Ball hog. You can't shoot," she said. I should've known she would turn on me. She complained every time the newspaper featured a teammate over her. Coach even reprimanded her after she mouthed off to a reporter about it. Gracie loved the spotlight, and I always wondered if it was because she didn't get it at home. Before every game, she looked for her dad. The few times he showed up, she played erratically, like she was trying to prove something, but the hurt pent up inside of her only clouded her decisions, resulting in turnovers. She quietly cussed him on our way to the locker room. It was rumored they didn't have a good relationship because he drank, but it seemed off-limits to talk to her about it.

Now, as I recall the things she yelled at me from the student section, I wonder if her words had less to do with me and more to do with the pain she harbored. Maybe if I had talked to her about the rumor, we would've become better friends and she wouldn't have said those things about me. Or maybe Gracie just needed to yell at someone, and it would've been me regardless. Every word she shouted seemed to cast the spotlight she so desired on her, and I just wanted her to shut up.

I launched a shot in front of the student section and missed. "Give the ball to someone else!" Zack said, earning Gracie's approval. I burst toward the hoop for the rebound, hoping to retrieve the ball so I could pound him in the face with it. Maybe it would rattle something in his brain that would fix his lisp. I wanted to scream at all of them, but I played like I practiced, acting as if their comments didn't faze me.

What I didn't hear on the court pierced me just as deeply. On Senior Night at the boys' basketball game, every athlete and their parents received applause except my parents and me. I had taken backlash, but when it affected my parents, my heart dropped into my belly. All of those years they spent coaching, cooking pregame meals, filming our games, and sharing in moments with parents in the stands, and this was how they were recognized?

Applause was also minimal at my last home game. When I was recognized with the other seniors, I was presented with flowers and a life-sized metal basketball full of cookies. My teammates smiled and laughed, but I dropped my head. Onlookers might have thought I was feeling sentimental about my last game, but all

I could think about was how my senior season wasn't supposed to end like this, with me wanting to throw the container and squash all the cookies.

• • •

Last season, fans had celebrated my three-point record and every point I scored. This season, I failed to deliver on their expectations. I used to be my team's most intense player. Now, I felt like I ran neck-deep through water, dizzy. Couldn't they see their discouragement affected me? I guess it didn't matter, as long as we won. After games, while my parents mingled, I crashed on the court, falling asleep until it was time to leave.

I wished to awaken to find that the season had been nothing more than a dream. In our district tournament game, we trailed by twenty with less than five minutes left. We scurried to narrow the gap, but our second state title run slipped away.

Janeen and I ramped up our efforts to keep our teammates focused. Since elementary school we had led our teams with energy. Our reputation for scrappiness worked both for and against us. When we outplayed our opponents, some girls pushed us, or when opponents beat us, they sometimes puffed out their chests or mouthed off. Janeen always walked away. I, on the other hand, usually had something to say.

When the referee whistled for play to stop, an opponent shoulder-bumped Janeen. "How do ya like that?" the girl said. She knocked Janeen off balance. I knew exactly how that felt.

"Give it a rest," I snapped. "You're winning, if you haven't noticed."

As I walked away, the referee whistled a technical foul. I just didn't expect his finger to point at me as he walked to the scorer's table. The call suffocated any opportunity for rebuttal. The buzzer sounded, and Coach substituted my teammate Kylee for me.

"Why'd you do that!" he said.

What does he think I did? The incident occurred on the opposite side of the court. He never asked me what happened or what I said, but he must have thought I cussed or talked back to the referee, and he wasn't the only one. The bench around me cleared. "I can't believe you," a teammate mumbled. Our confidence-deflated fans covered their mouths and crossed their arms, shaking their heads.

From mid-court, Kylee unleashed. "I can't wait until you're gone 'cause I can't stand you!" she said. Ever since she transferred to our school to play ball, I sensed her belief in her skills and resentment of mine. Once I left, she would play more. But I never knew just how much she wanted me gone until she belittled me in front of everyone. It felt like everything wrong wrapped up in one moment—from Amber's shoulder bumps to Mr. Littlefield suspending me to the homecoming pep rally mixed with Chelsea scolding me for dousing an opposing fan with my water bottle.

I wanted to storm center court and scream, "Didn't anyone see or hear what really happened out here?" But I kept still, thinking it made me less visible. I never would've guessed I'd feel so lousy for sticking up for someone. It helped me understand how my friends must have felt when they had defended me. Getting attacked for what we believe in can silence the best of us.

The horn sounded, and we headed to the locker room. "What were you thinking?" a player said, slamming her palm against a locker.

"Thanks for ruining our season," said a senior.

I wanted a state title as much as everyone else, but unlike them, I had lost more than a game. Despite their reactions, I knew what I had said. I knew that the technical foul didn't change the fact that we were getting beat the entire game. I raised my hand to Coach's to form our final huddle. Only Janeen joined. "Come on, get in here," Coach said, but the girls remained at a distance with their arms crossed.

"Why'd you do that, Tami?" said the same senior.

I jerked my hand from Coach's grasp. "This is what I get for sticking up for my teammate?" Surely Janeen would defend me. Like the time she gave it to a girl who was so annoyed by my defense that she smoked me in the face with the ball when I wasn't looking. I needed Janeen. I needed someone. I got no one. "Screw this school, because all it's done is screw me!" I said, fighting my bag strap away from Coach.

I re-entered the gym spewing the pain I had suppressed all year. Mom and my sister consoled me while our number one fan forced me into his embrace. He believed I was upset because we lost. A hug was the last thing I wanted, but I couldn't push him away. He touched me when no one else would. Dad tried to talk to my coach, but he walked away. I walked away too—from the moments in which I felt most loved and loved others so freely.

The next day, I stayed home from school and refused to go to the team banquet. An administrator told me I must be present or he wouldn't grant me my awards. He said it was a rule, although

I never found it in the handbook. A freshman player told me that when my teammates learned I wouldn't attend the banquet, they held a locker-room meeting where they agreed they wouldn't vote for me for any of the year's awards. "I wanted you to know because I don't agree with it," she said. She said even Janeen had voted against me. I wished I had never cheered so loudly or spent so much time with them. Their plaques held as much value as the homecoming tiara.

From my bedroom walls and dresser drawers, I stuffed the last of my spirit and pride into my team duffel bag, drove it to school, and hurled it into Coach's office. I didn't care if I ever saw any of my teammates again.

12.
THE LAST KNOCK

OUT OF ALL MY FRIENDS, Kevin bore the most burdens. Day after day, his shirt pockets absorbed my tears. "School won't last forever," he said. Kevin needed to believe those words as much as I did. I'm sure I'll never know the battles he fought for me. He knew telling me about that kind of stuff didn't help, and he certainly didn't do it for praise. He did it because that's what best friends do. I don't remember if I ever told him thank you. I thought we expressed our thanks by remaining present in each other's lives in everything we did, like when Kevin decided to change his image.

In the country, boys usually use their weight on the offensive line of the football team. They are our teddy bear Billy Bobs—those guys who lift the back end of trucks and pick daisies for their mamas. But Kevin never wanted to be known as a big boy or the guy who girls adored but never dated. Mentioning his weight brought him to tears. It was why, at our pool, even on the most humid days, he swam in a white Hanes T-shirt. After freshman year, he got fed up with people not noticing him, so he traded country-fried steak for grilled chicken salad and ran our road. He lost fifty pounds, joined the golf team, and our peers elected him to class office. He wore name-brand clothes and obsessed about the positioning of his frosted blond tips. Soon people noticed Kevin's swagger, and he scored his first girlfriend.

What Kevin lost in pounds he gained in haters. Some of the boys (especially the one who liked his girlfriend) said he had dropped pounds too quickly and gave him a hard time about his hair and clothes. The comments brought Kevin down, but I encouraged him not to listen to opinions. I was proud of him for improving his health and reminded him that he deserved the rewards he earned. Although his look changed and people started seeing him differently, I'd always think of him as the boy on my front porch, cupping his dirt-stained hands around his come-out-and-play eyes.

We hadn't fought since we were children, when I punched him in the arm so hard he cried and stomped home. Four days later, he showed up on my doorstep and into the woods we adventured. I never remember saying I was sorry. Thankfully, Kevin always came back.

I don't recall what brought Kevin to my door that bright spring day our senior year, but his frown told me he had not come to take me to the Tasty Freeze. Had someone given him a hard time at school? I don't even remember if I went that day. Had he covered for my skipping and got in trouble? Had I been insensitive toward him somehow? Or had someone offered him something he couldn't refuse, like an invitation to a party or a senior trip?

"What's up?" I said as I opened the door.

"I don't want to come in," he said.

I cocked my head like a puppy dog. I couldn't remember either of us rejecting an invitation into each other's homes. In fact, we went in and out of each other's homes so much our moms sometimes yelled, "Make up your minds!" My smile flattened. "What's wrong?" I asked.

Had I sensed what Kevin was about to say, I would've stepped outside to sit on the swing or grabbed hold of one of the porch posts. But there was no way to brace myself for what I never saw coming.

"I'm tired of defending you," Kevin said. "I just want to be popular."

"What?"

He walked away. I couldn't believe I was staring at this back. "Fine. Leave. And don't ever come back," I said, slamming the door, relieved the glass hadn't shattered.

"Whoa. Hey," said Dad, who jumped to the edge of his recliner at the same time Mom demanded to know, "What's going on?" My fear of getting in trouble for slamming the door mixed with resentment toward them for being just as blindsided as I was.

"I don't ever want to see him again," I said. I stomped to my room, fell onto my bed, and bawled harder than I had all year. How could Kevin do this to me? And why now?

Weeks earlier, he had moved to town. That was hard enough. As he settled into his new home, we were slightly more out of touch than normal. I thought we were trying to ignore the letdown of no longer living steps away from each other. But perhaps Kevin saw the move as an opportunity to shed his burden, like the snakeskins we used to find along the pool fence. I always wondered where those snakes slithered off to and why they needed to leave such an intricate part of themselves behind. I thought the worst part of the year was over, but as I replayed him walking down the sidewalk and driving away, it felt like the worst part had just begun.

Dad and Uncle Dave exploded over our split. They wouldn't speak for over a year. I still don't know exactly what was said, but Kevin told Uncle Dave a story that didn't match ours.

Over the following weeks, Kevin sold out to the Bees, but they still teased him about the effort he devoted to his appearance. "We're just joking," they said, and he played right along, although I knew it bothered him. Kevin knew better than anyone that if he didn't support their strategies, they would destroy his reputation just as they had mine.

If Kevin had died, I could mourn. Instead, my grief intensified every time I saw him with them. Why would he choose them over me? I didn't joke about his appearance. They weren't there to listen to him complain about his no-show biological father. They didn't put an arm around him after the garbage truck ran over his dog. They would never know him like I knew him. They wouldn't hang around after graduation or visit him at college. They weren't supposed to be in his wedding. Their kids weren't supposed to become friends with his kids. They were supposed to be with my kids, running all over the hills as Kevin and I had, continuing our traditions.

I never fought for our friendship, and Kevin never knocked again. His abandonment hammered me deeper than any other. I lost twenty-five pounds, and my pant size dropped from a five to a zero, changes I kept hidden under baggy T-shirts.

"Are you feeling okay? You don't look good," my friends and family said.

Mom suggested counseling, but I lashed out, certain a counselor would haul me to the psych ward. No doctor could fix my problems. I believed no adult understood; they just wanted to blame me. I had already asked for help. Adults had failed me. So, I'd figure out how to cope on my own.

I never wanted to cut myself, but I understood the idea of wanting to feel something other than what I felt. I tried to soothe my stings with a swig of tequila, but I choked on the burn. Wine coolers tasted better but provided no relief. I thought perhaps it would help if I changed my appearance. If I was unrecognizable, at least people might acknowledge me. I held my head over a sink and poured out bleach, but panicked when my hair sizzled. Thank goodness. Had I proceeded, I would've looked like a fried chicken. If only I were a guy. For boys, life seemed more manageable, hair and all. Unlike girls, they could fight and become friends moments later. No one held that against them. If I were a boy, I'd have been back in people's good graces by now. I never desired to become a boy, though. I wanted to stay true to myself. I liked who I was, but who would accept me? Outside of my family and a dwindling circle of friends, I trusted no one, so I kept to myself.

That spring I missed prom, numerous sporting events, the school play, three talent shows, pep rallies, and award ceremonies. Every day, I laid in my bedroom hugging my dog, who licked my face until I had no more tears to cry. Every night, I pleaded to God to let me fall asleep forever. I spent the night tossing in sweat-dampened sheets, falling asleep only after digging my fingernails into my scalp and pulling my hair. I awoke every morning to a locked jaw.

My grudges dragged me out the door but exhausted me in the long run. I drove to school, praying an oncoming car would hit mine. I became so despondent that I stopped paying attention. Once, I crossed our road to retrieve the mail and found myself quick stepping out of the path of a swerving, screeching truck. What if I hadn't jumped? What if the driver hadn't been attentive? The thought of dying scared me but not enough to jolt life back into me. What I was going through seemed meaningless, so I surrendered to a most dangerous place.

The darkest room of our house was our basement. Having watched one too many scary movies, I imagined creepy characters lurking in the corners. The furnace always seemed to kick on every time I was down there, sending me racing upstairs. But one day, the basement called, and I didn't even turn on the lights. I wasn't scared any longer, not because I was brave but because I was so apathetic.

Nothing and everything was wrong. I couldn't see beyond my wrecked reputation. I held no hope for new friends, a boy to love me, or a place and a people I could call mine. I burdened my loved ones. I ruined relationships for my friends and family. Others' unforgiveness weighed heavily, but my own weighed heavier. I could no longer take constant reminders of my worthlessness. Darkness beckoned my attention to the shotgun cabinet.

At the same moment I wondered how to load a gun, a beam of light shone through the window well, illuminating the clearest words I have ever thought.

Your life is not your own. Jesus died for you.

One radiant beam severed the enemy's grip, reminding me that God had created me in His image to honor and serve

Him, not for me to destroy myself. I thought about my family, about how wounding the people I loved most was not an option. Although I didn't yet understand the significance of those words, and although they didn't return a smile to my face or cause anyone to show up at my door asking to be friends again, I knew them as the truest truth instilled in the deepest part of me, and that was enough. I arose, unsure how to survive school, but certain I did not belong in the basement.

As often as possible, I stayed home. I used all my needed-at-home and illness excuses, missing thirty-three days. When I attended school, I considered a rampage, but exploding would prove that I was who they said I was. I couldn't let them win. If my enemies couldn't see me, they couldn't beat me. So I escaped to the locker rooms. Students were prohibited there during school hours, which made them an ideal hideout. In the darkest corner of the showers, the same place I used to pray with Janeen and two other teammates, I hugged my knees and overthought.

On and off for weeks, I wept in a toilet stall until a janitor asked me to return to the lunchroom. Instead, I snuck to my Chrysler LeBaron, the only convertible in the parking lot, its windshield a target for chewing tobacco.

At first, I just sat there watching my wiper blades clear the sludge, listening for the bell. But the more I escaped uncontested, and the longer no one seemed to care about my whereabouts, the less I worried about being caught, until one day I decided to leave whenever I wanted. Bailey promised to cover for me, but I found that if I slipped out during a class left unattended, or late enough in the day, no one questioned my absence, except the time I re-entered the cafeteria with McDonald's. "Where's mine?" said the lunch supervisor, who was also the chaperone who saw Amber shoulder bump me after prom.

"Sorry. I ate it," I said.

"Next time, bring me something. Will ya?"

Escaping was as easy as ordering extra fries.

13.
FINAL FAREWELL

I WALKED TO CLASS ALONE. My lunch table emptied. Underclassmen found other rides home, and boys who previously sided with me ignored me. Only a few months earlier, Kevin, Johnny, and Ethan had defended me when Zack passed around a petition to have me kicked off homecoming court. But now that Kevin and Johnny had bailed, Ethan disappeared too. In empty hallways, I walked by old friends who wouldn't even look at me. Betrayal led to denial. I became nonexistent, lower than the lowest.

I'm sure some of my schoolmates were influenced by others and didn't consider the consequences of their actions. Some of them probably believed their rejection was justice, sort of like when I thought I had the right to punch Tyler. I wondered if they would regret their actions later, but my main focus was how I would get through the day. As I counted down to graduation, I didn't think much more could go wrong—until it did.

Melissa and Kara tripped my panic switch every time they weaved their way from the opposite end of our longest hallway to alert me of who said what and how they had stuck up for me.

When they didn't see me between periods, they passed a note in the classroom or called me after school. Although I appreciated them sticking up for me, I didn't want to hear about every time someone rolled their eyes at the mention of my name. I contained my annoyance, but their voices began to feel like sandpaper in my ears, and I had to make it stop. At first, I responded to their gossip with, "So?" "And?" and "Whatever." But they didn't take my hints to back off, and Kara's nosiness was about to get the best of me.

Kara sat behind me in English when Mr. Brown called us to his office one by one to give us the results of our proficiency tests. "You failed four out of five," Mr. Brown said. "What happened?" I shrugged, wondering how he could be so clueless. I dreaded going back to class.

When each of us returned, the smartest kids in class inquired, "How'd ya do?" Every student talked about their passing scores, enlivened by dreams of scholarship money. I tiptoed to my first-row desk, ignoring Kara and the homecoming queen. *Why do they need to know?* Our teacher called us her special seniors, meaning she trusted us to talk quietly and play hangman on the board while she ventured to who knows where. I wished for her to bring an assignment, or a fire alarm, anything to rescue me, but the girls kept probing. "None of your business!" I said. Their eyes narrowed, and I immediately regretted my reaction. Why could everyone ignore me whenever they felt like it, but I wasn't allowed to ignore them?

The next day, Melissa came to my locker with gossip. "I don't want to hear it anymore," I said, raising my hand.

"Uh! Sorry you're in such a bad mood," she said, whipping her ponytail by my face. If I had said, "I appreciate you looking out for me, but I don't want to hear gossip any longer. It makes me feel sad," perhaps I could've helped the girls see I wasn't rejecting them personally. Maybe we could've set a different standard in our friendship. But that's not what girls usually do.

In eighth period, Bailey told me Melissa and Kara had called me a spoiled bitch. My chest caved. I wanted to believe the news wasn't real, but it came from Bailey. Even so, I decided to inspect the rumor on my own. That evening, I confronted them over the phone, individually, from the privacy of my room. My hands shook as I called Melissa. I worried I might blank when she answered, but I spoke calmly as I had practiced.

"Mind your own business," Melissa said.

"This is my business if you're calling me names." Dead air.

Impulsively, I called Kara. "I know what you and Melissa said about me."

"I don't know what you're talking about," she said.

"So how come Melissa just hung up on me when I asked her if you guys called me a spoiled bitch?"

"We were just joking," Kara said. "Gosh, don't get so fussy."

I reminded her of the names I had been called by people who hadn't been kidding. This time, I ended the conversation first.

The next day, I didn't plan to speak to the girls in our fourth-period history class, but I didn't expect to see them sitting on the other side of the room with Sara, Amber, Chelsea, and Dawn. I took my seat and turned my back. I should've remembered Melissa and the oak tree, that Melissa had always thrived on sweet nectar to create a buzz. My suspicion was finally validated.

"I can't believe she did that!" Sara said, shifting the attention of our entire class. The Bees rolled their eyes. A newspaper snapped and swallowed our teacher. Why couldn't Melissa and Kara have left our argument between us? Why did they have to involve them? It was the ultimate payback. They saved themselves from exclusion, regained camaraderie, and instantly realigned with the popular crowd.[14] I didn't attempt to understand. I only focused on how I'd leave that day.

An hour later, I arrived first at lunch, followed by Bailey, Rylan, and Annie. We had a long folding table to ourselves. Moments later, Melissa and Kara sat in their usual places, like nothing ever happened. Annie, who was with me in history class, stared with a gaping mouth. "Are you kidding me?" I said, throwing my arms overhead. "No. I'm not dealing with this anymore!" I grabbed my bag and headed for the door. "Now I know why kids bring guns to school," I said, catching the raised eyebrow of the lunch supervisor. He probably wanted his quarter pounder with cheese.

"Where's Mr. Littlefield?" I said as I flung open the office door.

"Out to lunch," the secretary said. I wanted to strangle him for not being there, for never being there.

"Tell him I'm not coming back," I said.

She gently guided me into his office. "I know how you feel," she said as she handed me a tissue and rubbed my back. I now know she was trying to be kind, but at the time her rubbing lit a fire between my shoulders. How could she possibly know what I felt? She didn't even ask why I was upset.

"Just tell him I'm not coming back." I marched out the nearest exit.

I gave the surveillance camera the finger and fishtailed toward home. The road blurred, but I refused to stop. I needed to be in my bedroom. On a winding state route, my tire dropped off the edge, and my steering wheel joggled. I closed my eyes, waiting to screech against the guardrail. Instead, my car glided back onto the road.

I tried to wipe the puffiness out of my cheeks so Mom wouldn't ask too many questions. "What are you doing here?" she said.

"I'm not going back."

"Do I need to call the school or write a note? You can't keep leaving whenever you want."

"I'm never going back. I just want to die," I said, shoving a barstool. I screamed and pounded my fist on the counter, spit and tears flying onto the carrots she was cutting for dinner. I ran to my room and planned to never come out.

"What do we do?" Mom said to Dad on the phone. "Can you just come home?"

As I pretended to sleep, I heard my door brush the carpet periodically. They called me to dinner, but I didn't talk to them for the rest of the day. As my family clinked their silverware, I scooted under my sheets and hugged my rumbling stomach.

During the early morning, I jumped awake. Nightmares weren't unusual, but this one confused my reality. Once I realized no one had thrown chairs at me in the school's gymnasium, I propped onto my elbow to face the repercussions of the dream. I smoothed my hair over my throbbing head. Had I been screaming? I wanted to wash down the scratchiness, but I spilled my water just like I had dumped my life. Why couldn't it stay in the cup, contained and useful? I couldn't open my mouth to take a drink anyway. My jaw was locked, so I flopped back onto my pillow.

The next afternoon, I sauntered to the kitchen for an orange juice remedy, sensing Mom's hesitancy to speak.

"You don't have to go back," she said. "Your doctor advised your principal to grant you a medical release."

"Who cares? Not like I need anyone's approval."

• • •

I'd finish the rest of the year from home. The dismissal required me to complete my homework by email. For the next month, only two teachers sent assignments, one from each. Looking back, I wonder if the faculty didn't know how to handle my situation, or if the administration even provided directions to them. As a teenager, I figured the teachers who sent work did so to appease my parents, and the teachers who didn't were glad to get rid of me. Bailey, Rylan, and Annie still received assignments. Why didn't I? I never thought I'd complain about not having homework, but not having homework made me feel more ignored. Mom called the school to ask if I had received all my work. The principal verified there were no further assignments for me, but he needed me to return to take finals in the guidance office. Located by the main door, he thought I could come and go without many people noticing.

Every day, I expected to awake relieved. Instead, I obsessed about my screwed-up life. Bailey, Rylan, and Annie distracted me better than anyone. On the weekends, they pulled me out of my room and into the safety of their cars, where we became the girls we should've been all year. Cruising town, we yelled at pedestrians and drove circles in the mall parking lot, hysterically laughing at our inability to do donuts. We blasted our music and bobbed to "Another One Bites the Dust" at red lights.

We probably looked like troublemakers to a lot of people, including the police officer who spotlighted us. Sure, we created some mischief, but really, we were four typical teenage girls just trying to escape the callousness of high school.

Bailey, Rylan, and Annie shared my anger as Kevin had, but we never specifically talked about what we were going through. I'm sure there were times my friends felt defeated too and perhaps resented me. But I never asked how they were holding up. In my weakness, they seemed strong. Why should I probe for rejection amongst three friends who still accepted me?

While at the time it seemed like everyone had abandoned me, I now realize I had more friends than I was aware of. Now I know some people backed away because they didn't understand what I was going through or how to help. Now I know some of them prayed for me, and I realize many of them checked out for reasons that had nothing to do with me. We were all dealing with something. Some classmates weren't around because they took courses at the community college. One of my classmates redecorated her room, setting up a baby crib at the foot of her bed. Another classmate spied on her mother, whom she suspected of having an affair. Some classmates prepared for military enlistment. Others had already signed apartment leases the day they turned eighteen. They had to figure out how to pay bills and buy groceries. Some had already been fending for themselves most of their lives. Others dealt with severe circumstances, like facing the choice to escape their parents' addictions or step into addiction themselves. One classmate emailed me years later and told me she dealt with her own bullies. I can't hold it against them for not being there for me when they were trying to figure out their own lives. Could there be a more awkward, confusing time?

Even so, Bailey, Rylan, and Annie were the only friends who stayed close when everyone else seemed embarrassed to be with me. The girls knew what I needed even when I didn't. They called me, came to my house, asked me to theirs, or simply sat beside me to stare at the clouds. Bailey invited me on runs. Rylan offered up a pile of junk so we could break things as a stress reliever. And when I said my final goodbye to my dog, Annie let me sob into her shoulder for hours. I'll never forget my friends' love and loyalty. It helped keep me alive.

The day after I left school, Bailey, Rylan, and Annie staged a food fight in my honor. They said the principal was angry but only scolded them for acting juvenile and made them clean up the mess. I imagined how good it must've felt to fling sloppy joe at Zack, and I was sorry I missed that. I appreciated the girls' stance, but weeks later, I noticed that their rebellion marked a turning point. With me gone, they returned to friendships with people like Kevin, Melissa, and Kara. People I thought had hurt all of us. While my friends deserved happiness, I felt secretly slighted seeing photographs of them dancing at prom.

Looking back, I see that our friendship seemed destined to fade, based on what they wrote in my yearbook. *I'm going to be lost without you,* said Bailey. We'd attend college two hours apart, but I assumed we'd call and visit each other often. I'd never thought of life without her. Rylan wrote, *I hope we don't grow apart, but if I face reality, that will probably be the outcome.* She signed off, *For the last time.* I didn't understand why we had to discontinue our friendship just because we finished high school. As much as I wanted to ditch my town, I never wanted to leave them, but it felt like they were ready to free themselves of me. Soon they'd graduate without the worry of how I'd wreck the day.

• • •

No way did I want to celebrate with people I hated, feeling hated, so I refused to take part in the commencement. Two weeks before graduation, Mr. Littlefield required me to write a note declining my involvement. If I failed to provide written notice, Mr. Littlefield said he would withhold my diploma. I knew another student who notified the school he wouldn't participate in graduation, and he wasn't required to write a letter. He was just ready to leave high school and get on with his life.

Why didn't the administration honor my wishes like they honored his? Was it Mr. Littlefield's way of making my messy year look tidy? Why did he need to control this? Did it make him feel powerful, one more way of sticking it to people who challenged him? Maybe he just didn't like us. He did work closely with the guys who had tried to give Dad a swirly in high school. Looking back, I wonder if he felt like it was the least he could do for me after not doing what I needed him to do most. I'm sure he genuinely wanted to see me enjoy that moment. Maybe he thought it would bring me closure. But at the time, it felt like such a hassle.

Mr. Littlefield also required me to return to school for photographs, and Mom and Dad agreed that I should. Grudgingly, I followed through to guarantee them a few cap-and-gown memories. I met Mr. Wilcox, a member of the school board, while classes were still in session for what was undoubtedly the oddest graduation ceremony in the history of graduations. Walking through the hallway, I stood out like a cherry in an empty sundae dish.

The photographer snapped a few shots, and I willed myself to smile just like I had during homecoming. "Where are you going to college? What are you going to study? How's their basketball program?" Mr. Wilcox said.

Who's he trying to fool? He doesn't care.

"I think she just wants to get out of here," Mom said.

He shook his head. "Between you and me," he whispered, patting my shoulder, "Tyler got what he deserved." I felt like giving him a few "between you and me" comments. Instead, I tucked my diploma under my armpit and quietly cursed the place to Hell.

• • •

I never planned to go back, but that summer I returned to condition for college basketball. As soon as I stepped onto the track, my legs felt lassoed to the shelter house. After two laps, I stomped on the inner lane and beat the air. "Why am I here?" I screamed through clenched teeth. I walked across the field to leave, but my memory tripped at the forty-yard line.

Junior year, Janeen, Gracie, and I passed this spot on our way to ring the victory bell. That year, we painted our faces every game and ran the school flag across the sidelines. Us tomboys got a kick out of people saying we were more entertaining than the cheerleaders. I looked to the field house, where I once curled as much weight as a girl who wrestled sheep. I couldn't straighten my arms for a week. There was the hill where I received my first kiss from Ethan. Sara had been ten feet away, kissing the boy I had liked since preschool. At the softball diamond, a ball had popped off another player's foot and bloodied my nose. The dugouts swirled as I hit the ground. Echoes of my coaches calling, *Are you all right?* floated onto the football field, where I felt as busted as ever. "Why did I even go here?" I said. "I hate this place!" I dug my fingers into the ground and ripped up sod, kicking a fifty-gallon trashcan on my exit. I vowed never to return. This time, for good.

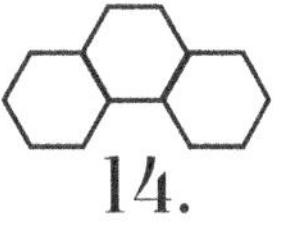

14.
GOD IN THE GLOW STARS

DISOWNING A BUILDING is easier than closing the door on a pulsing past. I used to roam the fifteen-mile radius I called home looking for familiar faces, open to meeting new people. Now I focused only on where I needed to go and the task in front of me. To lessen my chances of seeing people and being seen, I boycotted the mall and drove back roads. But as hard as I tried to distance myself, I couldn't prevent scrutiny.

"Why did you drop out?" my grocery store cashier classmate said. "Some moms are saying you're pregnant." Out and about, people glared or rolled their eyes. Students gagged, flipped off, pointed, laughed, and mouthed off at my family and me. Across the gas pump, harsh looks replaced handshakes. Whispers greeted us in restaurants. "You need to get over it," said Dawn's mom to my mom, approaching her in the grocery store like nothing ever happened.

Years later, at one of my speaking engagements, someone asked, "Why didn't your family move?" Human nature searches for the quickest route out of discomfort. Had my parents left the choice to me, we would've revamped our lives elsewhere. My parents, however, had learned not to make rash decisions at the most emotional moments. They maintained composure, modeled resiliency, and avoided airing their frustrations in front of me. When their reactions didn't mirror mine, I retreated, unsure why they made me go through any of it.

They could've made my life easier. After I punched Tyler, they could have negotiated a lesser punishment. They could have demanded that my administrators discipline my aggressors. Every time I came home upset, they could've allowed me to take the next day off. They could've agreed to let me transfer or home-school. They could've swooped in to fight my every battle, but they didn't. Instead, they told me to suck it up, for themselves as much as for me.

As a teenager, I didn't comprehend how agonizing that year was for my parents. They exhausted resources only to end up tangled in red tape. As desperately as they wanted to remedy the situation, they couldn't. They stressed over whether they were doing the right thing, carrying that stress behind closed doors, into nightmares and visions of retaliation. Watching life leave a child's eyes is enough to make any parent want to go ballistic. The pressure became so overwhelming that Mom sought professional help for anxiety.

Had I known how my actions would impact my family, I would've acted differently.

None of us could've predicted the outcome of that year. We could only accept what had transpired. Starting over in a new place might have made life more comfortable, but what a disservice it would've been had my parents sheltered me from conflict. They toiled to provide the stable home they didn't always have as kids and earned us the right to remain rooted upon the land we loved. Opinions wouldn't drive us away. "Suck it up" reminded me that life is unfair, people are sometimes unkind, and I'm not entitled to lose control of my emotions or run away when things don't go my way. As much as I resented the discipline at the time, weathering criticism prepared me for the harsh world ahead.

I still wonder how many friendships would've survived if I had never thrown that punch and how many were destined to fade regardless. In hindsight, I know that not everyone rejected us. I wonder how our responses may have caused others to think we were unapproachable. We could've tried harder within our community or sought friendship two towns over in any direction. But in a place where reputation precedes introductions, rebuilding our social circle was daunting. Ultimately, we kept to ourselves, quietly adjusting to our altered social landscape.

I once hosted a party that filled our yard with more kids than my parents had initially allowed. Friends invited friends, and I cringed at every unplanned arrival, certain my parents would declare this party my last party. But they didn't turn anyone away. They grilled more hot dogs. That was the last time they would ever worry about running out of food.

The spring after my senior year, eleven friends attended my graduation party—Bailey, Rylan, Annie, and eight guy friends, of whom all but two were either older, younger, or attended another school. I didn't expect anyone to come uninvited, but Janeen and two teammates showed up. I never saw the girls before Dad asked them to leave. "I don't think the timing's right tonight, girls," he said. Why did they come? Maybe they hadn't planned on stumbling upon my party, or perhaps someone invited them, and I never knew. I never ran out to the driveway to see what they wanted, and they never returned.

I never thought I'd enjoy having teammates sent away from my home, where we had gathered for pre-game meals, sled riding, and pool parties. Out of everyone, Janeen left me with the most memories. The first time she visited, we fished. Her brown eyes widened as she braced her sixty-pound frame, reeling in the biggest catch I'd ever seen from our pond. Our dads lifted the catfish onto the dock, but before they could warn Janeen, she jerked her hand from its electric whisker. When her tears receded, I lifted her off the dock and we headed to get first aid.

After our final game senior year, I needed her to lift me. More than anything, I wanted her to speak, forgetting that ever since that day on the dock we had comforted each other not with words but through touch. When I ripped my hand from hers in that last huddle, I didn't care if I ever saw her again.

Eight years later, Dad called with the news. While Janeen was working on a home renovation, the toxic fumes of a generator overwhelmed her. She never made it out of the basement. I think Dad expected to console me, and as I pictured Janeen lying there, I wasn't sure why I didn't need it. Her family held her funeral in our high school gymnasium. I heard the place filled with more fans than we ever attracted to any game.

I used to wonder what was wrong with me. Why had I never cried about the death of a friend I once loved dearly? Now I know that sometimes we grieve for people just as deeply when they are alive as when they are dead.

• • •

The summer after senior year, my parents considered a lawsuit. They met with two representatives of the school district, who apologized for my experience but said administrators were unaware of my problems. The representatives felt no changes were necessary and assured my parents the school district didn't fear repercussions. Again, my parents asked me to go to counseling. I agreed. Counseling would support our case, expose my school's negligence, and help Mattie and other families that might face similar circumstances. Most of all, I hoped to punish my school.

The only thing I knew about counseling, I had learned from television. I swore I wouldn't lie on a chaise lounge and whine about my feelings. Neither would I reveal too much to the doctor, fearing she'd have me hauled to the loony bin.

I pulled down my hat bill as I entered Dr. Sheridan's waiting room, greeted by gossip magazines, certain that any doctor who subscribed to tabloids couldn't possibly help me. When she called me to her office, I parked it in a La-Z-Boy, taking in photographs, dream catchers, and figurine-lined bookshelves. "Okay, tell me why you're here," she said. Her trinkets lowered my defenses, but not enough to speak. "Begin whenever you're ready," she said. I thought I might get away with saying nothing, but over the course of ten minutes she continued to coax me. "You know you're going to have to talk to me, so you might as well start," she said.

"I'm here because my parents might sue my school," I said. "I had a really bad year."

"Sounds like you've been through a lot," she said, handing me a box of tissues. "What happened?"

I tiptoed back to the oak tree. Dr. Sheridan's curiosity compelled me to spill more than dry facts. She interrupted only to clarify who was whom and who did what. "That's terrible . . . That must have been upsetting . . . Then what did you do?" she said. She even giggled when I told her about punching Tyler. "Well, he deserved it," she said, quickly placing her hand over her mouth as if to say whoops. "Of course, now we know we can't do that. But go ahead, keep talking." I'm still not sure whether she actually agreed with my action or if she was just using reverse psychology. Coming from a doctor who subscribed to gossip magazines, maybe it was both. Either way, I think she knew what she was doing—gaining my trust.

For the first time, someone accepted my story without scolding me. It was exactly what I needed, but I couldn't continue. Overwhelmed by Dr. Sheridan's empathy, I plucked another tissue from the box. "It's okay. We're about done for today anyway," she said.

Dr. Sheridan lived and worked outside of my community. We didn't know the same people. This, combined with her compassion, helped me feel less judged, and I trusted her enough to speak more freely during our remaining sessions.

Insurance only covered six appointments. I'm sure more would've been helpful, but the amount was just what I needed. Over the course of my next five appointments, Dr. Sheridan reminded me that if I wanted to heal, I would need to continue to process my experience beyond our sessions, and I knew I would when she left me thinking about what became the most important thing I could think about. During my final visit, Dr. Sheridan concluded, "It seems as if there's a spiritual void in your life."

"Void?" I shrugged. "What's that mean?" I regretted my vulnerability. Surely, she had saved reprimanding me for now.

Instead, she repeated my statements and helped me see my issue was no longer with people but with God.

In all my schooling, I only remember asking, "Why do I have to do this homework?" and "When am I ever going to use this?" I learned that good girls don't challenge authority. They submit to the process without interruption. I listened, I memorized, I filled in the blanks, and the system rewarded my lost curiosity. I left unable to solve the most significant problem school had presented. But now, for the first time, I heard myself think.

How could I disconnect from God and not realize it? I called on Him when I needed help, said my prayers at bedtime, and read my graduation devotional, which reminded me of His love. But if God loved me, why did He let this happen? Why didn't He protect me? I was supposed to carry my foundational friendships with me for the rest of my life, if not practically at least fondly in memory. No matter where I ventured, I was supposed to look forward to returning to my roots, where everyone knew my name and welcomed me home. Why did He take away the place and people that served as the center of my life? I thought He wanted me to act nicely and stand up to meanness. How could I have been so misled? I no longer understood my value, where I fit in, who I was, or who I was supposed to become.

Frightened by the realization, I drove home and stomped into the woods. "Why did You do this to me? Why didn't You help me?" I swung at the air. "I hate You." For weeks, I struggled to make sense of what I had been through. Convinced God punished me for enjoying popularity, I continued into the woods to unleash until I quieted. Every day, He beckoned me to a hillside, where I practiced praying like I practiced playing. In basketball, if I missed more than two shots, I shot fifty to a hundred more. It didn't matter that the security light buzzed, Mom had called me in for dinner, or I was tired. Similarly, when negative emotions and memories surfaced, I prayed harder and longer. The more I prayed, the more I reflected, and the more I felt God in my words. Some days I only said "Help" or "Please don't let me feel this way," and that was enough. Or I simply listened to the breeze brush the trees and knew He heard me. When I finished, I didn't leave Him outside. I couldn't. God saturated my thoughts, following me to bed, where I imagined Him in the glow-in-the-dark stars on my ceiling and talked to Him until early morning.

As summer ended, so did my parents' pursuit of a lawsuit. "It's over. We need to move on," they said, advice I refused to accept. I didn't understand that they feared losing money fighting a court battle and thought it would cause further damage for Mattie, who didn't want to change schools. She didn't want to leave her friends, and because most of my bullies' siblings would be gone by the time she entered high school, my parents felt she would be okay to stay. She would have the same administrators and teachers, though, and a lawsuit could've affected the way they treated her. At the time I was mostly concerned with how they treated me. I thought I'd find healing in seeing my school punished. I thought if I said my prayers and read my devotional, God would quickly reward me with retribution. But if God wouldn't give me the answers I wanted, I wouldn't let go. So, I boxed up my bitterness and loaded it onto a moving truck.

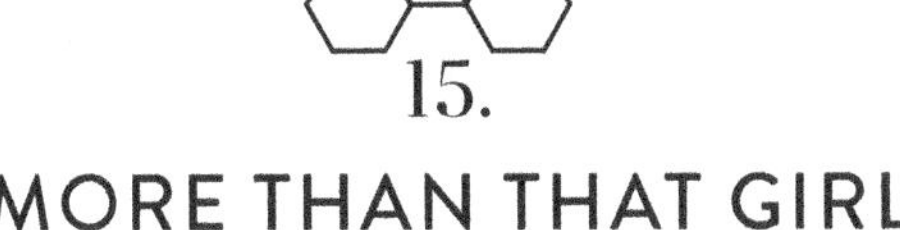

15.
MORE THAN THAT GIRL

NO ONE FROM HIGH SCHOOL attended my college, but that didn't stop me from unpacking my past onto people I didn't know. Instead of focusing on good experiences with girls, I braced myself for conflict. How was I supposed to live with roommates? I heard stories about girls whose disagreements escalated to hair-pulling and throwing each other's belongings out the window. What if that happened to me? Or what if my roommates and I liked each other at first, only to repeat what had happened to me in high school? What if they hogged the closet or left messes? What if I confronted them about annoyances and they retaliated? Would they ignore me? How could I live with people who wouldn't talk to me? What if they twisted my words to make others believe bad things about me? What if they scrubbed the toilet with my toothbrush, destroyed my belongings, or did stuff to me in my sleep, like give me a black permanent marker mustache, or chop off my hair, or smother me with a pillow?

Over the summer, I talked to my future roommate Maria on the phone. She seemed personable, giggling after every comment, but so much could change in person. Relief came in knowing my other roommate, Katie. In high school, we had played two seasons on the same summer basketball team and would play as college teammates now. The summer team we played on wasn't as close as my other teams, so Katie and I had much to learn about each other. She and I would share one of our suite's two bedrooms. Earlier in the year, Katie's dad had passed away, and our families thought we could comfort each other if we bunked together. I felt valued that someone might want my support, but what if I couldn't help? What if Katie took her pain out on me? If she didn't like me as a roommate, would she influence our teammates? What if I didn't fit in with them either? What if my new teammates picked up where my old teammates left off?

The more I imagined my roommates turning trivialities into major problems, the less I considered issues with girls as what-ifs. Girls would set the tone for one of the most important transitions of my life. Despite my worries, I never entertained an alternative. No matter where I went or what I did, the possibility of rejection awaited.

First to arrive to the dorm, I double-checked the room number. It couldn't be right. I didn't belong here, surrounded by concrete block walls. My throat tightened. My greatest source of reassurance was at home, bedridden with a broken ankle, leaving Dad and me to move in. We turned on player-coach mode and began executing the game plan.

After a long day of holding on, we let go. I stood in the doorway, tempted to run after him, wanting him to tell me one of his spontaneous bedtime stories like he did when I was five, to ease my mind and make my room feel less scary. When he left, I crumbled inside, but before I could outwardly unload the weight on my chest, Katie and Maria sought me out to ask about my stuff, which made me curious about them too.

Katie decorated her desk with pictures of her dad and filled us in on her boyfriend, whose photograph she taped to the wall. Maria's room looked like a sunshine explosion of smiley face stickers, posters, pillows, tchotchkes, and positive affirmations. She overused the phrase "thank you so much," which scratched at my nerves but also drew me to her. Liz, a sophomore basketball teammate, later filled a vacancy and became our final roommate.

First semester, Katie appeared to hold up. Although she left globs of toothpaste in our sink, our lifestyles meshed, and we became more than teammates. Maria and I met for meals, took study breaks for chocolate milkshakes, and occasionally traveled home with each other on the weekends. Liz assumed the role of our mother hen, and we freshmen welcomed her advice about which boys to steer clear from. The four of us shopped, painted our nails, gave ourselves facials, and swapped clothes. We danced and sang loudly around our room and decorated to celebrate each other's birthdays and test scores. Through numerous late-night laughing attacks and secret sharing sessions, I paid less attention to shielding my heart.

As new friendships developed, old friendships faded. Bailey spent most of her time with her college friends, and Annie and Rylan soon married their hometown sweethearts and started families. Although we'd never reunite in the same way, those girls set the standard on which I'd base every friendship for the rest of my life. My roommates would never replace my best friends, but Liz, Katie, and Maria proved I could look forward to the best relationships yet to come.

The safety of our circle helped me reclaim confidence outside of our room. My smile re-emerged, I welcomed conversations, and I joined the school newspaper and Fellowship of Christian Athletes. By the time I met my basketball team, I relied less on worst-case-scenario survival skills and enjoyed a fresh shot at a new social scene.

At our first meeting, the girls reunited with high fives and hugs. "Quiet," said two seniors. Another eagerly checked off the agenda's bullet points. A sophomore rolled her eyes. Liz walked in late. As punishment, the upperclassmen demanded she dance. She busted out moves to their handclaps, and they quickly forgave her. Although I couldn't keep up with Liz on pre-season runs, I followed her lead as I assumed my role amongst some of the most competitive girls on campus.

In the workout center, after I knocked over a rack of weights in front of the boys' team and the girls hassled me for making a freshman mistake, I wanted to crawl under a bench, but I realized that laughing made the situation more enjoyable. When the girls saw I rolled with their teasing, they gifted me the nickname "Shorty" and invited me to dinner. Every time I matched their efforts during training or answered their peer pressure, I earned more admiration, like when I agreed to partake in their drunken scavenger hunt and performed a humiliating skit in front of everyone at halftime of the soccer game. After our last run, they officially marked me one of them by cracking an egg over my head and dunking me in a lake.

Just as Liz had shown me how to earn my team's acceptance, my teammates showed me how to earn recognition across campus through partying. On spinning dance floors, my insecurity swirled out of my mind. No one cared who won homecoming queen. They didn't hold my family history against me. They couldn't punish me for mistakes they didn't know about. No one disliked me because of the cars my family owned. They didn't make fun of my long hair, friendliness, clothes, or the way I played ball. Without interference from the past, I befriended all kinds of people, from international students to beer-guzzling fraternity brothers and bongo-playing hippies. Hearing my name called out while walking to class reignited my addiction to acknowledgment, and this time I wasn't going to mess it up.

However, when conflict arose between three of my teammates, the past crept in. Problems within the girls' love triangle poured into practices as two of them refused to pass the ball to the other, who eventually exploded. Their arguments created tension amongst our whole team, but my other teammates only talked about the situation in their absence, and our all-female coaching staff ignored it.

I avoided the conflict, but soon one of the girls approached me to take sides. "I don't want to get involved," I said. "I just wanna play ball." Whether or not I wanted to participate, the girls didn't leave much choice.

As the season approached, my teammates thrived on more drama. Captains held meetings to identify players who squealed to the coaches about our partying. "We're not starting practice until someone fesses up," they said, pointing fingers at specific players. When the star of the team feared drug testing, she compelled other teammates to cover for her whereabouts before she went MIA. And when players ventured outside team boundaries—for instance, if a girl attended sorority events over team activities—upperclassmen mocked her behind her back but within earshot. "We're the only sisters you need," they told me during rush week.

Players who controlled team dynamics learned from a coaching staff that coerced players to adhere to the organization's unwritten rules. Although my major was journalism, my coach served as my academic advisor. Admittedly, she knew nothing about journalism and pressured me to change to exercise science because, she said, it was what all players majored in and best suited an athlete's schedule. She also recommended I add a class—women's studies. "You should learn about feminism because it will help you gain an appreciation for women like us," she said. I shifted the focus to my journalism courses, but she circled back, making her suggestion seem more like a requirement. "All female athletes take women's studies." I wasn't sure what "women like us" meant, but I trusted my coach and figured the class would help me better understand girls' complicated dynamics.

Two weeks into the class, right as I was beginning to trust my gender again, my perception of females was challenged. The professor lectured on family structure, explaining single-parents, same-sex parents, extended family, stepfamily, and the nuclear family. "Who here belongs to a nuclear family?" she said. Out of a class of over thirty girls, I raised my hand alone. "Why do you think you belong to a nuclear family?" she said.

"Because I don't belong to any of the others."

She spent the remainder of class prying at the intricacies of my parents' relationship. "Who earns the money? Who pays the bills? Who physically holds the checkbook?" she said, rolling her eyes and increasing her harshness after each of my answers.

Classmates joined, frowning on the fact my mom didn't run board meetings and my dad didn't cook. The more I defended my family, the harder they came at me. "You aren't from a nuclear family," my professor said. "There's no such thing as a nuclear family. You aren't who you think you are."

I never left a class feeling more violated than I did that day. In my first weeks at school, I was optimistic about rebuilding, but this incident made me feel beat down by more bullying and left me questioning what I was even doing in college.

When I relayed my experience to my coach, she said, "Good, maybe it will encourage you to be more open-minded." I didn't understand how my traditional upbringing automatically made me close-minded, but I soon learned "women like us" meant "think like us or sit the bench." These women preached tolerance while their actions denied me my uniqueness. The game pieces didn't change just because the playing field advanced. Power-trippers exist in every setting.

Just when I lowered my guard, my worries became realities. I knew I couldn't spend four more years exerting my energy for teammates who wouldn't pass the ball if they were angry at me and coaches who wouldn't do anything about it. So I quit. I told myself I wasn't running from opposition but readjusting my priorities. Now I realize it was both.

After twenty years, I finally understand that what happened to me that day in class was the culmination of the attack on my identity. Who was I going to allow to tell me who I was? So many times I've replayed going back. If I knew then what I know now, I wouldn't have cried one tear over their judgment. I would've stood on my chair and told them, "It doesn't matter what you think of me. I know who I am!" But in that moment, it did matter, and I didn't know. Now I can see God's proclamation playing out: *Your life is not your own. Jesus died for you.* Because I knew that, I knew it wasn't up to anyone else to tell me who I was or who I wasn't. God created me in His image, and that meant He was in me, and I was in Him—God was my identity.

Although I sat in class silenced for the rest of the semester, conviction stirred within me. Despite my struggle with self-confidence and belonging over the past year, I knew who I was and where I came from. I was more than a basketball player, more than a student, more than a girl defined by others' opinions. I wouldn't compromise my identity to make my peers or professor feel more comfortable. I just needed to figure out how to express myself as I began learning the difference between belief and faith.

16. NAILS AND WOOD

I FILLED THE SPACE left by basketball with books, but what I looked for I wouldn't find in a classroom. I hadn't missed a Fellowship of Christian Athletes meeting since I quit ball. Even though I no longer played a sport, I fit in there more than anywhere, surrounded by people who challenged my thinking without berating who I was. Every week, pastors and athletes taught expected lessons: Don't drink; don't do drugs; dedicate yourselves to God more than sports.

Just when I thought I had heard it all, I met a man whose message confronted me more than any other. As I approached the meeting room that day, I wondered if I had missed a cancellation memo. Peeking in, I caught the buggy-eyeballed warnings of two members. Following their line of vision, I understood why.

Russ Clear was six-foot-three, 310 pounds, with a shaved head and twenty-two-and-a-half-inch biceps. Donning a steel chain link necklace, he reminded me more of a heavy-metal, head-banging, iron-pumping drill sergeant than a preacher. I thought about tiptoeing out. I had just finished a brain-straining week of classes. I didn't feel like kicking off my weekend with this dude's sternness. However, leaving wasn't an option. Russ spotted me, and something connected me to him. I couldn't walk away.

Russ's story made me appreciate my worst days. Born in a Southern Californian neighborhood run by the Mexican Mafia, Russ seemed doomed from the start. To escape the pain of emotional, physical, and sexual abuse, he turned to drugs and was first arrested at eleven years old. As a former Hell's Angel and Aryan brother, he survived gunshots, stab wounds, a crystal meth addiction, and suicide attempts. He spent fifteen years in America's roughest prisons. During his last six months in San Quentin, he turned from darkness to devote his life to Jesus. With transformed strength and power, he spent the rest of his life conveying the gospel to thousands by breaking cinder blocks with his head, baseball bats over his knee, and twisting metal rods into pretzels. The intensity of this never-back-down, six-time world champion weightlifter commanded my attention, but his vulnerability captivated my heart.

Russ retrieved a nail from a five-gallon bucket and—*BOOM*—drove it through a two-by-four with a single punch. Jolts rippled through the room. One kid spilled his water. Russ grabbed another nail and—*BAM*. Somehow, it felt appallingly familiar. Once more, Russ picked up the board and another nail, gathered an immense amount of force for what appeared to be the blow of all blows—but his fist stopped shy. Out of everyone, he looked at me, as if he saw the hatred I secretly harbored. Still before us, he bowed his head. Beautiful tears streamed the burliest face. Out of violence came peace. I stared, dumbstruck.

I had never ridden a motorcycle. I had never even smoked a cigarette. At five-foot-two, I didn't look intimidating. Russ and

I contrasted in every way, yet we both knew broken trust. We had been failed by people and had failed people. We were two people so wounded that we wounded others. We served our punishment. And although Russ had faced physical bars, I was more imprisoned.

With his board and bucket of nails, he spoke of how Jesus gave up everything, even the love of God, to die for everyone's mistakes because He loved us so much He wanted to save us from destruction. Russ approached each of us with his bucket, asking if we would confess our sin, accept Christ as our Savior, and allow Him to lead our lives. Everyone who agreed took a nail to a makeshift altar, the windowsill, to pray. Even though I gave my life to the Lord when I was nine, I said yes. With nails and wood, Russ embedded Jesus within me in a new way.

At the windowsill, I watched a weather front engulf the parking lot. My mind whirled, but I dared not move, afraid that someone would see the puddle on the shelf before me. The shadow of the impending storm crept up my shirt. Rumbling brewed within. When I could no longer control my whimpers, I erupted and scurried to the hallway, where my legs gave out. I would've laid there all day if Maria hadn't met up with me. Since I had stopped playing ball, Maria and I had become best friends. Katie and Maria even switched bedrooms so Maria and I could spend more time together. There in the hallway, she soothed my sobs and held me up as we walked back to our room.

For the rest of the afternoon, I zoned out on our futon. No one willingly sat on that cheap thing, but I didn't even notice its prodding. I only replayed Russ driving the nails through the board, imagining Jesus's pain. A twinge traveled down my arm—Christ's arm. Flexing the tendons, I cringed as I heard the pop of His punctured flesh, iron ripping through nerves. The heaviness that pulled Jesus downward on the cross compacted me into a ball of regret.

• • •

For the past two years, I thought no one understood. Although some of my friends expressed empathy when I shared my story, I still hadn't connected with anyone who shared an experience like mine. Russ reminded me that Someone understood my hurt like no one else ever could.

Jesus knew both cheering crowds and whispering critics. He foresaw His rejection, and at times, He got riled up. He took a stand, calling out corruption by overturning the tables in the temple courts. Not everyone agreed with His actions, especially those in power. They felt so threatened they tried to trap Him in His own words. They spread lies and manipulated others against Him. People badmouthed and laughed at Him. When they didn't like what He had to say, they ran Him out of town. Association risked reputations. Friends abandoned Him. Peter denied Him, not once but three times. Judas sold Him out for thirty pieces of silver. Although Jesus knew his friends would turn on Him, He still loved them, even when betrayal rocked Him.

Every heartbreak that happened to me had happened to Jesus first, but what I experienced paled in comparison. While I sought popularity, Jesus chose the bottom of the social ladder, allowing Himself to become despised, "like one from whom people hid their faces." (Isaiah 53:3) He sacrificed His reputation to save others. I only wanted to protect myself. When people ridiculed me, I exploded. Jesus never uttered one word in retaliation. I hated my bullies. Jesus loved His. Even while His enemies crucified Him, He pleaded, "Father, forgive them, for they do not know what they are doing." (Luke 23:34)

I had treated God casually, but I expected Him to take me seriously and fix my problems promptly. I had told Him I hated Him when life didn't go the way I thought it should. I remembered pouring bleach on my hair because I thought if I changed my appearance, I might regain acknowledgment. It wasn't until now, as I sat on the futon picturing Jesus bloodied and beaten, that I realized He had become unrecognizable so that I could be seen, always and forever. The revelation of His righteousness and my badness clobbered me. My mistakes nailed Him to the Cross as much as anyone's, yet He died the death I deserved, absorbing my deepest shame. Who was I to deserve such love? My lack of reverence ripped at my heart. At that moment I'd have given my life to have been His substitute, but all I could do was pull a blanket over my head.

The following evening, I drowned my shame with a bottle of Mad Dog, staggering back to people for the kind of love only God could give.

Awaking with a blank memory, a sore butt, and a churning stomach, I returned to the futon, the nails, and the board. All day I was emptied of my superficial saviors. In my discomfort, I begged for forgiveness, finally finding what I searched for—resurrected royalty, the Redeemer of my rejection.

17. ELEVATOR RIDES

I COULDN'T DENY THE SHIFT inside of me, and it wasn't just that my stomach didn't function properly for the next three days. I should've sought medical care. I turned to my Bible instead. In the index, I looked up words like *gossip*, *rumors*, *betrayal*, and *trust*, which connected me to stories that reminded me I wasn't alone. What happened to me had happened to people since the beginning of time.

When Aaron and Miriam wanted the power Moses had, they spoke against him.

When Joseph shared his dreams with his brothers, they envied him, gave him the silent treatment, conspired against him, and handed him over to the enemy.

Because people praised David, King Saul tried to kill him. Saul's hatred infected others, igniting a war between families.

When Nehemiah set out to rebuild Jerusalem's wall, a clique ridiculed him and spread lies, hoping to ruin his reputation.

Flipping from story to story, I saw how the characters of the Bible faced rumors and disloyalty. They agonized over lost friendship and community. They often faced conflicts more extreme than anything I had experienced, but they forced me to consider my challenges. I saw how they failed and triumphed in their responses, and how, in despair, they sought God's healing and protection. I wanted faith like theirs, but my grudges blocked me from moving forward. Scripture nudged me to reflect and showed me how to eradicate my bitterness.

Every time I came across a verse about forgiveness, I squirmed. I wanted words that cushioned my feelings. What I found didn't always justify what I felt but called me to evaluate my heart and live my faith. The Bible said:

"If you forgive men when they sin against you, your heavenly Father will also forgive you. But if you do not forgive men their sins, your Father will not forgive your sins." (Matthew 6:14, 15)

"And when you stand praying, if you hold anything against anyone, forgive him, so that your Father in heaven may forgive you your sins." (Mark 11:25)

"Forgive, and you will be forgiven." (Luke 6:37)

"Be kind and compassionate to one another, forgiving each other, just as in Christ God forgave you." (Ephesians 4:32)

"Forgive whatever grievances you may have against one another. Forgive as the Lord forgave you." (Colossians 3:13)

I knew that forgiving was the right thing to do, but how could something God required feel so excruciating? I wrestled with it for weeks. Like when Dad traveled for work to improve our lives, I knew if I wanted my circumstances to change, I had to do things differently. I was tired of rediscovering happiness only to cycle back through anger. Forgiveness was freedom, and I knew I could achieve it because I saw others do it. I not only saw my parents forgive each other after they argued, but I saw them forgive a close friend who betrayed them multiple times. And I read other peoples' stories, including a Holocaust survivor who forgave a Nazi solider. The more I listened to others forgive things that seemed so unforgivable, the more determined I became to follow God's plan. Through all my moans, I forced myself to read the verses aloud. At first, they stuck in my mouth like cotton.

"God, you really expect me to do this?" I said after squeaking out the words. I agreed only out of obligation. The more I read the verses, the stronger my conviction grew and the more fluid the words became until I said what I never thought I would: "I forgive them. I forgive Sara. Chelsea. Tyler. Mr. Littlefield. Melissa. Kara. Kevin."

With every name I released, I lightened from my face to my fingertips. The lifted weight made room for the peace I craved. As I welcomed conversation between God and me, the process became doable, even enjoyable—until another party joined.

• • •

I thought apologies would help me move forward. Kylee's thrust me into the past. My former teammate, who stood at mid-court and screamed at me during our last basketball game, emailed me while I was at college, expressing regret for her actions. I had worked so hard to release myself from that moment, and in seconds, her email reignited it. Initially, I considered blasting her so she would know how much she had humiliated me. But what would I accomplish by adding wrongdoing to the situation? I removed my hands from the keyboard.

I could withhold mercy and unravel my progress, or I could give her grace like Jesus gave me. I never expected to feel so unworthy as I re-read her words. I replied by accepting, and with one click, I lost the need to receive any more apologies.

While forgiveness provided peace for the past, I would need practice to apply it to the future. When I returned from Fellowship meetings, I shared my excitement with Liz, Katie, and Maria. They all believed in God, and I thought they would join me at campus fellowship, but they never seemed too interested. Liz accompanied me once and decided she didn't like it. I accepted her decision and understood we didn't have to participate in the same activities. Yet, the more I grew in my faith, the less enthusiasm I received from my roommates, until they eventually stopped speaking to me. At first, I tried not to take their behaviors personally. But weeks passed, and as I overheard them cheerfully talking to each other and everyone except me, I felt like an outsider.

One afternoon, I peeked into Liz and Katie's room and noticed they had taken down our photographs and replaced them with pictures of people I didn't know. I rationalized a redecoration in progress, but weeks later their walls looked the same. My image was nowhere. Why were the girls acting this way? Was my excitement annoying? My growth unrelatable? Did I talk about my new friends too much? I hoped my roommates didn't feel forgotten. Just in case, I gave them more attention, purposely entering a room to acknowledge them. When I heard one of them leave for class, I tiptoed to the elevator, squeezing in through the closing doors.

"How's your day?" I asked.

"Fine."

"What are you up to?"

"Studying."

"What are you doing this weekend?"

"Going home."

The instant we reached the ground floor, they burst out.

Ride after ride, I asked the same questions and got the same minimal responses. The nicer I acted, the farther away the girls pushed me. When I entered the fitness center or dining halls, they turned their focus to someone or something else, and when we saw each other on the walkways, they quickened their pace or changed direction. It seemed like I couldn't do much more but watch my fears unfold.

What did I do wrong? Why couldn't we get to the point? Why couldn't I go to them and say, "Hey, I notice things have been different. Can we talk?" Because confronting the girls would force me to face the same devastation that wrecked me before. I couldn't bear it, not again. As much as I wanted to end the tension, I backed off and prayed for the predicament to resolve. But the longer I stayed quiet, the worse things got.

After we returned from Christmas break, Maria left school, leaving Liz, Katie, and me with a roommate vacancy for the following year. We threw out ideas of who to ask and began our search. Because Maria and I shared a bedroom, I tackled our problem with urgency, locating a replacement within a few days. Neither Liz nor Katie raised objections about our new addition, a freshman named Hayley. After our first collaboration in months, my hope arose. I filled out my paperwork and assumed my roommates would do the same. I never questioned our plans until I ran into our neighbor Beth, Liz and Katie's teammate.

"Who are you rooming with next year?" she said.

"Liz, Katie, and Hayley."

Beth's expression sank. "Sorry to tell you this, but Liz and Katie are gonna live off campus with some girls on the team."

I took two hard swallows, but that queasy crying feeling expanded. Unlike my reaction to Tyler's rumor in high school, I paused. I wish I could've blamed Beth for stirring trouble, but I knew her as honest. The story explained Liz and Katie's behavior, although their bailing on our agreement seemed like a convenient escape from something more. It was time to find out what. Did they think if they didn't tell me it wouldn't hurt? If they gradually distanced themselves from me, life between us would go on as usual? If the rumor was true, they had left Hayley and me in a jam, having to make frantic changes to our housing paperwork, which was due the next day.

I flung open a door closed far too long. Liz lay motionless on her top bunk. "We thought you made other plans," Katie said.

"How could you think that when you guys haven't talked to me in forever? We had an agreement!" I slammed the door, shutting out some of the only people I had felt safe amongst since high school.

My roommates knew what I had been through. Why would they add to it? Although I never considered their behavior bullying as much as compounded miscommunication, I still felt like the girl who used to lock herself in a bathroom stall. I couldn't believe I had fallen for friendship again. Their abandonment reinforced the idea that I couldn't trust girls. The only way I knew how to deal with them when they hurt me was to tell them off and ignore them as if we had never been friends.

• • •

Weeks later, I got stuck in the elevator with Katie. I couldn't push the "close" button rapidly enough before she slipped in. Sure she had stolen my trick, my jaw tightened. Tension swelled. I thought of how we came to live together and wondered how two heartbroken girls could comfort each other only to turn around and inflict pain on each other. When we arrived at the ground floor, Katie offered me a ride to class. I don't know why I accepted. Later I realized this was God within me, nudging me to make a decision I would never have made on my own. This became our routine twice a week for the rest of the semester.

We could've taken the stairs, but we kept riding the elevator. It was always only the two of us, and it felt like our conversations couldn't get more awkward. Unlike Katie's usual mellow demeanor, she blurted out sentences like she was playing a childhood game that required her to pull her hands back before getting smacked. I could tell she was trying and thought maybe that was her way of apologizing. Every ride, she strung together more sentences until they became relaxed. As the elevator lowered, so did my defenses. I reciprocated more and began feeling bad that I had blown up and slammed our bedroom door.

We never said too much on our rides to class. We didn't socialize outside of our trips. Neither of us said, "I'm sorry," and we never reopened our bedroom door. We never talked about what happened, but every time we stepped into the elevator, I learned more about what forgiveness really looked like. That sometimes it doesn't happen with words but with actions, and that it isn't the same process for everyone. When Kylee apologized, it was easier for me to respond to her email because I'm better at expressing myself through writing than talking. Forgiving Katie was more like forgiving Tyler after his email threat, but it was also different because I didn't expect Katie and I to become friends again. And we never did. But I knew I had forgiven her because I released her in a way I had never released anyone. I no longer carried the hurt she caused me, and I hoped she felt as freed as I did.

18.
A VISITOR'S GRASP

THE DEVIL WHISPERED, *Don't trust girls*, but this time I didn't run away. I immersed myself in the company of my fellowship group, where meeting after meeting I witnessed girls embrace each other's difficulties. When I walked into the room frowning after my falling out with Liz and Katie, four girls met me in my circumstances, and I knew I could confide in them. They didn't probe for details or run to others to incite drama. They listened, placed their hands on my shoulders, and prayed, their touch serving as a reminder not to punish all girls for the offenses of a few.

Week after week, the girls invited me to meals and on walks and knocked on my door to say hi. One evening after we left fellowship giddy, I tripped and caught myself on my friend. I looped my arm around hers, and we joked about rolling down the hill to the dorms. "If we roll, we roll together," she said with her fist in the air. I felt secure knowing someone was willing to fall with me. But as we parted ways and I walked to my room alone, heaviness washed over me. I didn't fully understand it in the moment, but now I see that it was the same kind of heaviness that sat me on the basement stairs my senior year of high school. *You shouldn't be having this much fun*, I thought. *Something's wrong.* Now I recognize that those thoughts were not my own, but I took possession of them. I scolded myself for talking too much and laughing too loudly. I analyzed why I shouldn't have friendship. If I hung out with my new friends too much something about me was bound to cause a problem. I warned myself not to get too involved because the times I had been attacked were the times I had been having the most fun.

I wished I could return to the book basket at the library, where I'd secured my best friend simply by asking, "What's your name?" and having a mutual interest in the Berenstain Bears. But, I remembered, I didn't remain friends with the girl from the book basket. She had traded me for Sara without warning at the start of junior high. The memory sounded an alarm. There was no reason to punish my new friends for what happened in the past, but I felt a sudden intense need to distance myself from them.

If only I could find one friend who would never disappoint me, a friend who embodied the innocence of my biddy ball teammates, the adventure of Kevin, and the loyalty of Bailey, Rylan, and Annie. I wanted one friend who knew my thoughts before I spoke, a friend who answered when I called, who made a disagreement feel more like an agreement, and whose fondness didn't fizzle with distance. Was that too much to ask? In a world of imperfection—yes. The kind of friendship I wanted, no human could give.

It was the first time I truly realized only one relationship was guaranteed to uphold when the rest failed. Only God could provide me everything people couldn't. He listened every time I called on Him. He cared like no one else and wanted the best for me, always. He planned to prosper me, not harm me, and give me hope and a future. (Jer. 29:11) He was the best friend I could ask for. Through memories of betrayal, the devil tried to pull me away from friendship, but it backfired when God showed me how to become best friends with Him.

• • •

I understood what it meant to let Jesus into my heart. My mom had taught me that my conscience was the Holy Spirit living within me, but I had not yet learned how to connect with God through more than silent prayers and church activities. The liveliest moment in my childhood church was when our children's choir sang "This Little Light of Mine." Mostly, we sat with our hands folded, turned to the pages marked in the bulletin, and stood when the pastor asked. On the rare occasion anyone let out an "Amen," it startled the rest of the congregation. Church seemed more like a visit to the library.

While there is value in stillness, my fellowship group showed me new ways to encounter God. When we sang, my friends' voices boomed. Even if they were off pitch, it didn't matter. They released with all their might because, no matter how it sounded to us, it sounded beautiful to God. They lifted their hands, clapped, jumped, bowed, or sat in prayer while everyone else sang. No denominational rules restricted them. They only focused on celebrating God in their own ways, but together. I had never participated in anything like it. It was what some people, including myself, considered extreme. I had always thought hand-raisin' and loud praisin' were for religious fanatics, what we called Holy Rollers. I thought praying during singing or asking questions during a pastor's sermon was disruptive, but as I studied worship, I learned none of that was weird—it was Biblical. What was extreme was the amount of basketball I played. Extreme was punching people to express myself and downing a bottle of liquor to feel accepted. It didn't make sense that I could pump my fist and woo-hoo for sports or dance at a party but sit unmoved for God. This missing component of my faith was like friendship without laughter; it was God and Jesus without the Spirit. I couldn't know more of God without experiencing the part of Him that lived within me, the part that gave me words when I didn't know what to speak and made me move when I felt stuck. The part that would come close to me if I came close to Him. So I stopped holding back.

Amid the flicker of candlelight and soothing strums of acoustic guitars, I set aside my insecurities, lifted my arms, and belted out some of my favorite songs—"Open the Eyes of My Heart," "God of Wonders," and "Did You Feel the Mountains Tremble." Reaching for God connected me with a power I had never felt before, a power that welled within me like a war cry for a battle I couldn't lose.

By prioritizing God as my most important relationship, my focus shifted from how badly people had and could hurt me to how greatly God loved me. I wanted to encounter Him in everything I did. I walked across campus less worried about how I looked and more appreciative of the air I breathed, sunshine, flowers, and the rain that nourished them. Before every meal, I bowed my head no matter who sat at the table. I changed the music I listened to, attended parties sober, and surrendered my desperate need for a boyfriend. I applied a spiritual perspective to my studies, which I shared during class discussions. When I learned my body was a temple of the Spirit, my workouts became an act of worship. People noticed the change, which started conversations. I shared my faith with my family, and we returned to church. For the first time I could remember, I lived unrestrained by others' opinions because I lived more fully for admiration I didn't have to earn. As I sought God's Spirit, my motives became richer, and my life flowed with proper order. I felt a deep-rooted confidence I had never experienced before. My grades improved. Even my love life fell into place when, a semester later, I started dating the boy who would become my husband.

• • •

After an evening at fellowship, I bounced to my room, where moonlight called me beneath my windowsill to pray. Staring out, one of hundreds in my five-story building, I imagined I looked so small to a God so big, but I knew He saw me and heard every word. An hour later, I forced myself to study, but after reading the same paragraph three times, I tossed my book on the floor and scooted to the edge of my chair. I closed my eyes to thank Him, but words weren't enough. Like the nails and wood from my futon meditation, I needed something more, so I retraced in my mind Christ's steps to Calvary.

The air was thick with fury. Pebble-pelting, spitting spectators lined the narrow street. Jostled within the mocking mass, I caught a glimpse of Jesus, blinded by blood, staggering under the crossbeam. My heart plunged. I had to reach my Savior. By the time I fought through the crowd, I could do nothing more but sift through His trail, stretching my ruby-stained hands toward the honor I didn't deserve.

Although I had locked my door, I was not alone. Someone snuck in who put me at ease. As my guest moved closer, goose-bumps rushed my limbs. Tears traced my cheeks. I dared not peek. I didn't want to lose the moment. Wrapped in security, saturated in bliss, I felt a shockingly familiar touch. The words that once gripped me on the basement stairs—*Your life is not your own*—became the grasp of He who now held my hands. I gasped. He let go, but I knew He would never leave. Best friends don't abandon each other.

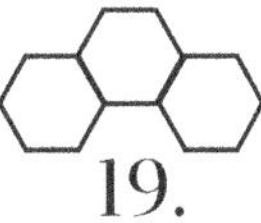

19.
THE TROUBLE WITH GIRLS

HAYLEY AND I ENDED UP LIVING in the oldest dorm with my geology classmate Meghan and her sorority sister Stephanie. The bonus to having hammer-banging pipes and ghostly creaking floors was a larger-than-average corner room. None of us knew each other well, but everyone seemed nice enough to share a bathroom.

Optimistic about the year ahead, we socialized most during the first month. But as we settled in, Meg and Steph did their thing, and Hayley and I did ours, together and (more often) individually. The separation felt natural. As an upperclassman I buried myself in books, devoting most of my free time to my boyfriend and exercise. The real world lay just ahead, and I needed to prepare. My get-it-done, task-oriented personality couldn't have contrasted with Hayley's demeanor more.

Whenever I told Hayley I was going to work out, see my boyfriend, or go home for the weekend, I had the feeling that she rolled her eyes and stuck her tongue out once I turned my back. As though she really wanted to say "And?" or "Good for you," and not the "I'm happy for you" kind. When I returned from a run, she'd point out that sweating was icky and running sounded horrible. When I came back from fellowship group excited about a new song or a friend I had made, she'd reply with, "Hmm." I thought I was being considerate and practicing safety by letting her know where I was going. But in hindsight, I sense I annoyed Hayley as much as she annoyed me, and I wonder how many times we resisted expressing our true feelings about one another.

When I returned from morning classes and saw Hayley still in bed, I won't deny that I slammed the microwave door harder than normal to wake her up. She'd wipe the sleep from her eyes in a theatrical gesture and retreat to the couch with a bowl of cereal to watch television until it was time to head to her two-o'clock class. It drove me nuts that I had to strain to complete my assignments while it seemed like Hayley never worked too hard. She glided through the days, careful not to take on too much. If she did, she became frazzled. At least once every week her mood plummeted during phone calls with her boyfriend, at whom she screamed for an hour. I sought quieter spaces when tension spiked, and I avoided hanging around her with my boyfriend—we didn't fight like they did, and I had a history of girls holding my happiness against me.

Whenever I felt irritated with Hayley I took a breath, grateful she had not walked out on our plan. In less than a year I'd live in a senior single, where I wouldn't worry about adjusting my personality or schedule to meet others' needs. But when you live with someone who imposes on unspoken boundaries, everything from their snoring to the way they scuff their feet and chew food can make a year seem like an eternity.

The problems between Hayley and me began halfway through the year, around the same time that Hayley's mom faced a health crisis. I felt for Hayley. She lived hundreds of miles from home and wouldn't see her mom until a school break. When she told me, I listened and offered a hug. Weeks passed, and Hayley talked to me about her mom only once. She appeared to hold strong, which should've been my indicator that things were not as fine as they seemed.

One evening, for the first time that school year, we both studied at our desks. Preparing for a long night, I put on pajamas, grabbed twelve ounces of caffeine, and settled in to translate legal jargon into a twenty-page term paper for a class I could only pray to pass. I had procrastinated, and the assignment was due the following day. So far, I had accomplished more complaining than writing, while Hayley fussed about her sociology assignment. "Wanna trade?" I joked, pressing my palms against my temples.

Less than an hour into our work, Hayley stretched. Away went the books, on turned the television, and out came the cereal. "You're done already?" I asked.

"Eh, I'll finish tomorrow," she said, nesting into the couch under a blanket. "Tiffany and Julie will be here any minute."

Hayley informed me her friends' television was on the fritz, so the girls needed to gather in our room to watch their favorite show. *Social time while I'm straining my brain?* I should've objected. Instead, I remembered compromise was part of living with others. *It's one show,* I told myself. *I can deal.*

An hour later the show had ended, and I no longer tolerated the mix of three giddy girls and a blaring television. I slammed my pen. *Don't they know how important it is that I finish this?* I sighed loudly. *How do they expect me to write with all this noise?* I cocked my head, casting my disapproval in their direction. They attacked their popcorn bowl like hyenas over hors d'oeuvres, oblivious to their mess.

"Is your television fixed yet?" I said.

Their chewing slowed to a stop.

"No," Tiffany said sharply.

I popped in my earbuds, determined to use the mental toughness Dad taught me in biddy ball. Seconds later, I jerked at the slam of our door. The girls had turned off the television and left. An hour later, they had not returned. I still had no idea how I'd finish my paper, and I was sidetracked from scolding myself for waiting so long to start it. My busted brain needed a shock. Perhaps a cold shower would awaken my productivity. En route to the bathroom, something caught my attention—a note under the crack of our door.

All you ever do anymore is study and spend time with your boyfriend. You never have time for me. You're no fun. You're mean. You're negative. And Tiffany and Julie see how rude you are to me! The note went on to say that I ruined their entire evening because they couldn't watch any other shows. The three of them would be in Tiffany and Julie's room if I wanted to talk.

Although I never raised my voice with the girls, I could've asked more respectfully. I assumed they realized they were being inconsiderate. Maybe Tiffany and Julie didn't know that Hayley had informed me of their gathering only minutes before they entered. They probably had no idea about my paper. I never told Hayley no. I shouldn't have expected her to know my irritation. Maybe she had more confidence in me than I had in myself to finish the paper. Perhaps she thought I'd take a break and join their good time. Or had she sensed my vulnerability and intentionally staged drama? What was certain is that we miscommunicated.

I had no idea Hayley felt this way. There must have been underlying reasons that set her off. Initially, I defaulted to the typical "girls are jealous" response because in her note, she seemed to hold my happiness and pursuit of success against me. I wondered if she compared the stabilities in my life to the instabilities in hers, because they were obvious to me. Perhaps she attacked the areas in my life that were most deficient in her own. When I look back, I realize there could've been many reasons for Hayley's reaction. Maybe it had less to do with envy and more to do with what she didn't relate to or had no desire to understand. Maybe she struggled with her mother's illness more than I knew. I had no clue what kinds of grades she earned. Maybe they weren't as good as I thought. Perhaps Hayley considered us better friends than I did and expected more availability from me than I ever knew. At the time, she hung around with Tiffany and Julie so much that I assumed she received the support she needed. I didn't know what stressed Hayley. I was zoned in on my life and didn't devote much attention to her. As much as she annoyed me, I never meant to hurt her—but I had.

Like many girls, Hayley confided in her inner circle rather than tackling her issues head-on. In doing so, she addressed her frustrations to everyone but me. Hayley knew my anger toward Liz and Katie. Perhaps venting to her friends, rallying their support, and sliding a note under our door seemed like the safest way to communicate, but to me it felt so middle school.

I already didn't trust the girls. When a classmate wedged the bumper of her car into my wheel well and a tow truck had to pry it off, I got fired up and spouted off in the privacy of our room. Although I cooled down quickly, Hayley wasted no time conveying the situation to Tiffany and Julie, who in turn embellished my anger to my classmate. "They said you hate me," my classmate said. Insurance would repair the damage to my car, but it wasn't as easy to convince my classmate that I didn't hold her mistake against her.

The note smoldered in my hand as I thought about the girls talking behind my back again. I had sixteen pages left to write that weren't getting written, and now this problem further blocked my thinking. I needed to take care of it, ASAP, so I could get on with my work. I crumpled the note and stomped out the door, blinded by the fact that a three-versus-one confrontation wasn't going to land anyone anywhere but hurt.

All of a sudden, I stood before Hayley, defending myself against her accusations. Tiffany and Julie joined the reprimanding. As the shrillness of Hayley's voice sliced through my nerves, my fists clenched. I needed to exit. "This is why I'm not friends with girls like you," I said with a scolding finger. They quieted, and I strode away to take the walk I should've taken after I read the note.

The wind cooled me. *Why couldn't they simply apologize for being loud? Why are girls so dramatic?* The harder I walked, the more I loosened. *Why did I need to argue with them? Why couldn't I just let it go? What did I accomplish besides proving my anger and burning three more bridges?* I couldn't stand the cold any longer. I'd search for answers after I took a hot shower and pounded out the rest of my paper.

When I returned to my room, I walked in on Tiffany telling

Meg and Steph half-truths about things I said about them. I calmly asked her to leave and tried to repair the lies. Meg and Steph assured me they held no harsh feelings, but time would show Tiffany's damage. Soon enough, the girls walked to class and ate meals together. Meg no longer talked to me unless I spoke to her, keeping her responses short and punctuated with eye rolls. Why did girls live for the gasp-and-gossip? Why were they so easily turned against each other? Girls drove me crazy.

• • •

Talking to someone outside my situation had helped before, so the night of our argument, I approached our residential advisor, Diane, to ask if she would mediate. Diane was a senior. Between her age and her position, I thought she could offer wisdom. If Hayley and I had someone to encourage us to deal with our conflict, maybe we could decipher a normal disagreement from a personal attack, respond differently, and arrive at a solution. Wasn't that how mature women handled disputes? However, Hayley had already met with Diane, who informed me that I caused tension because I was too direct.

"I can't help," she said, throwing her hand up. "I just don't relate to you." Her partiality baffled me. Would she have listened if I had slid a note under her door? I felt like I was fighting the Honeybees 2.0, sent away by Mr. Littlefield's protégé.

Too direct? What did she mean I was too direct? I thought indirectness had caused our issues. Hayley and I could have told each other in private what was bothering us instead of reading between the lines and letting our emotions stew. What I believe

Diane meant is that confrontation between girls is off-limits. Girls aren't supposed to yell it out. It's more acceptable to tiptoe around conflict, gossip with friends, call another girl names behind her back—anything but what I did. While not incapable of indirectness, girls like me who handle their problems directly often come across as unnatural, abrasive, and insensitive. Ironically, in an environment that touted girl power, I felt like my voice was dismissed because it didn't mirror the average.

• • •

Withdrawing from girls seemed like the safest way to steer clear of petty issues. So, I stopped attending my fellowship groups, where I engaged with girls most, and I started hanging out with my boyfriend and his basketball teammates.

With them, I felt more at ease, maybe because they reminded me of the boys I grew up with, maybe because there was less pressure to talk and less analyzing. I didn't necessarily want to sit around and debate sports, but neither did I want to tread through a landmine of feelings. When I asked the guys direct questions, I got straightforward answers. When they asked for my opinion, they knew they'd receive it, and they wouldn't twist it to demonize me. If they said something insulting, I could shoot right back, and they'd still talk to me the next day, knowing I was angry but allowing me to be angry. And they apologized quickly, sometimes without even understanding what they had done.

Socializing with boys seemed safer, but it wasn't foolproof. I knew of guys who gossiped and manipulated as much as girls, and I had been bullied by males. However, I knew girls to be more passive-aggressive, which had caused the majority of my troubles. No matter how others acted, I needed to figure out a better way to express myself and nurture my relationships.

Whenever I felt attacked, everything inside of me happened so fast. New attacks zipped through the past, attaching to moments in which I had felt most wronged, inciting my defensiveness and driving my confrontations. I thought going off on adversaries sent the message "you can't do that to me," but trying to control how people treated me only made my problems worse and fueled my unforgiveness. I could blame it on my bloodline or being bullied, but neither forced me to take ownership of my actions.

• • •

After our residential advisor refused to help, I turned to our campus counseling center. "Why do girls act this way?" I said to the counselor. "Why does this keep happening to me?"

The only answer she ever provided was, "I don't know. What can you do about it?"

"I don't know," I said. "That's why I'm coming to you. Why doesn't anyone ever have an answer for stuff like this?"

"I guess it means you have to figure it out on your own," she said.

My lips tightened. I snatched my bag and vowed to never return to the counseling center. My irritation fueled my walk back to my room. *If no one wants to help me figure this out, fine. I'll figure it out myself.* I grabbed my Bible and turned to "anger" in the index. I flipped to James 1:19: "Be quick to listen, slow to speak, and slow to become angry." I read it until my furrowed forehead smoothed, knowing those words were meant for me. God was calling me out. I didn't like it, but I couldn't just close my Bible and make those words go away. They seared into my mind, and I had to accept them.

Now I realize the verse wasn't about denying anger or avoiding all problems. Instead, it encouraged me to deal with my emotions properly and use my directness wisely. God gave me spunk not to suppress it but to use it in a way that glorified Him and honored others. The keys to slowing my anger were surrendering my impulses, studying Scripture, and reflecting in prayer. God gives me the strength to restrain myself and discretion to know when and how to speak up. But at the time, I didn't understand all of that. I just knew I needed to keep putting myself in situations that required me to slow my anger, even when it was uncomfortable. And if I failed doing what I believed was right, I didn't need to feel ashamed for trying to improve.

I hadn't liked the outcome between Liz, Katie, and me, and I didn't want the same with Hayley, Tiffany, and Julie. Although I no longer wished to socialize with the girls, I hoped this fallout could end with mutual understanding, built on the forgiveness I had learned on my elevator rides with Katie. With James 1:19 on my mind, I talked to Diane again and asked for her mediation.

"Hayley wants nothing to do with a resolution," she said through her cracked door. "Just leave it alone."

For the first time in four years, a door closed that I didn't feel the need to pound down. I walked away filled with peace.

• • •

I left things alone, but Hayley seemed intent on causing more aggravation. The night of our argument, she had agreed to move out, unofficially filling a vacancy in Tiffany and Julie's room. But she resisted finalizing the paperwork, prolonging the process for months.

While Julie distanced herself from the conflict, Tiffany tried to kindle animosity. If Hayley needed something in our room, Tiffany retrieved it while I was gone, leaving me sticky notes that told me I was "stupid," "childish," and to "get a life." I refused to participate in more drama, so I tossed her notes in the trash. According to the residential department, I couldn't stop her from entering my room, but I wasn't going to allow her meanness to distract me. My not-reacting must have irritated her, because her next move was sending me similar unprovoked messages on social media. When I blocked her account, her campaign finally ceased.

Returning home from the library one evening, I found Hayley socializing with Meg and Steph. When she heard me enter, she scampered to our room. We exchanged hellos, and I made the mistake of starting our conversation with a request. A couple of days prior, Hayley had failed to relay a message to me, resulting in a scheduling jam. Unsure whether she hadn't told me out of spite or forgetfulness, I politely asked her to please remember next time.

I saw no reason for Hayley to flip out. I recognized a problem and wanted to fix it. Wasn't communication the key to any relationship? Unfortunately, I had only considered myself. My timing couldn't have been worse. Had I considered Hayley's personality and opened with casual conversation, I might have helped her relax instead of giving her a reason to detonate.

Hayley's arms flailed like a mad orchestra conductor, throwing clothes and books in a pile and a shoe at me. I couldn't console her. I leaned into our bathroom doorframe, mesmerized. Why couldn't we work through our problem? Why did we bury our hostilities until we either ignored each other or exploded? After her you're-so-this and you're-so-that outburst, she slammed our heavy bathroom door, nailing my shoulder. My face was burning as I looked at my reflection in the door's thick coat of lacquer. I had a decision to make. I could run out the door and chuck the shoe back at her or stay put and do what James 1:19 told me. I cautiously cracked the door, taking inventory of the mess, wondering if what just happened was over. Would Hayley return with Tiffany? As I gathered Hayley's belongings into a mound, I worried that the worst-case scenarios I had invented about roommates before I entered college would come true that night. Surely, I'd wake up with my hair hacked off.

Hayley's pile remained untouched for the next three days. I went home for the weekend, and when I returned, her things were gone. "Yes!" I said, pumping my fist. She had officially moved in with Tiffany and Julie. I immediately rearranged my room and enjoyed the rest of the semester in my own space. I only saw Hayley from a distance a few more times for the rest of college, and I never saw her again after I graduated.

I wish we could've sat down and talked before she moved out, but I'm also okay that we didn't. Because we left things as they were, my relationship with Hayley became the defining moment when I finally learned that not every action required my reaction.

20.
DEFY THE LIES

I'D SURRENDERED MY RIGHT to participate in high school commencement, so I looked forward to my college graduation, where I'd finally stride across the stage to the cheers of my family. When the day arrived, girls swayed to sorority songs, teammates huddled, and roommates embraced, capturing scenes they would show to their kids years later. They would become each other's bridesmaids, weekend getaways, and favorite throwbacks on social media. I watched them walk away with the kinds of friendships I had only managed to wreck. How did something I used to thrive at become such a disaster? I turned my tassel, bid farewell to life's main avenue of camaraderie, and embarked on the rugged relational road ahead.

After school I tried making friends at my job, but socializing with coworkers felt forced. At tailgates, volunteer events, and conferences, I met nice people, but our conversations didn't extend past brief encounters. I turned to church, the wives of my husband's buddies, business networking events, and social media, but it seemed like everyone already had friends, friends they had grown up with, the kind of friends they invited to dinner and showed off on their newsfeeds.

I had heard the advice "if you want a friend, be a friend," but for some reason that philosophy didn't work for me. I could prove it through mounting rejection. The harder I tried to find friends, the more out of place I felt. I tagged behind my husband at gatherings, never totally one of the girls, never totally one of the guys. Although I talked more easily with guys, I avoided speaking too long because I didn't want to send them the wrong message or raise their wives' eyebrows. It wasn't that I avoided females; I just talked to them more cautiously, stuttering along in anticipation of them twisting my words.

The slightest negative encounter fed the lies that fueled my anxieties. Before I met people, I invented reasons why they would misunderstand me. I looked for uninviting body language and listened for whispers. I latched hold of any remark I perceived as insensitive and embellished it for days. "Told you they wouldn't like me," I said to my husband as we left events. I expected relationships to fail, and what I expected, I attracted. Meanness hurt less when I saw it coming, and envisioning rejection validated rejection when it happened.

Gone forever were effortless conversations, roaring laughter, voices that called for no particular reason, places that were my places, people who were my people. I viewed the whole world as my bully, punishing many for the behavior of a few. I complained about reckless drivers, people who didn't say "excuse me," unreturned smiles, broken commitments, and unfulfilled promises. As "I'm busy" became a modern mantra and no one seemed willing to look up from their phones, it was easier to disengage than to bother people, and it protected me from disappointment.

I stopped calling people who never answered. I stopped sending party invitations to people who rejected them. I became self-employed and maintained a small clientele. I gave up attending church, backed out of family functions, avoided conversations, and chose self-service machines over human contact.

The less I interacted, the fewer problems I faced with people, but the more my issues ballooned. As I scrolled through photos on social media of young women with their friends, I wondered, *What's wrong with me? I'm such a turn-off. No one wants to be my friend. Everyone already has friends. I'm not worth anyone's time. I don't relate to anyone. I don't fit in anywhere.* This loss of control over my thinking contaminated my spirit and my interactions with others.

• • •

Every summer, as my family sat poolside, it was Dad's habit to plan cookouts for upcoming holidays. Gathering friends was easy when I was a kid, but as a young adult who still hadn't figured out how to manage the pain of rejection, I didn't know how to get back to that place. "Who are we gonna invite?" I said. "I don't have any friends."

"Go make some," Dad said.

"How? It's not easy for me like it is for you."

Most of our family friends were Dad's business connections. It was wrong of me to assume those relationships were easy for him. Now I know some of them presented him with challenges, challenges I wouldn't have handled as graciously. But at that time, I secretly relied on him to keep our social lives afloat while I complained about how difficult it was to make friends, and how once I made them, I couldn't keep them, like Abby, who had recently dumped me.

Abby and I had been casual friends since middle school. In high school, she joined a program at the nearby community college, so I don't remember seeing her much my senior year. We reconnected after school, when her best friend abandoned her, and she needed someone to talk to. We met for dinners and hung out at her apartment, and I grew hopeful. But when Abby's best friend re-entered her life, I was disposable. And hurt. I wrote her an email about how I felt, but she never responded. "I can't trust anyone, Dad," I said, reminding him about Abby. "Why even try?"

The more Dad talked about having parties, the more I thought about the friends we used to have, and how it had all disappeared. Fourth of Julys and Labor Day weekends passed, and we didn't have those cookouts, but Dad never gave up hope that we would, and it made me angry. Angry at people who never had time or always had something better to do. Angry at myself for screwing things up for my family, for not knowing how to fix it, and for not being a better example to Mattie, who had started struggling with friendship during college. And angry at Dad for trying, because I felt like it further highlighted my failure. I should've comforted Dad when his invitations were rejected, but I rubbed it in more. "See? People suck," I said. "Stop trying."

My heart sinks when I think about having said such a thing. Now, I would never tell my dad to give up on one of his top strengths. It's one thing I love about him—his relentless love for people, which holds me accountable to keep extending my hand.

But as a hurt young adult, the only way I knew how to process rejection was with my mouth.

When he repeatedly tried to connect with people who always said no, I would say, "Well, I don't want to hang out with them anyway." I said it out of hurt, for myself but also for my family. Now I realize that I often allowed one no to overshadow multiple yeses. I can think back to friends who welcomed us to birthday and Christmas parties and to those who would've been at our house after one phone call, but in our distrust, we pulled away from them.

At the time, my perspective was so clouded, I couldn't see that people who said no probably weren't rejecting us as people. Maybe it really wasn't a good time for them, or their priorities were actually more important than us, or maybe they were putting up their own boundaries, careful not to get too close to the boss's family. I didn't entertain their reasons. Instead, I fueled my family's resentment until they adopted the same language. We'd sit around the pool and complain, and I'd feel better in the moment because my family shared my pain.

"Death and life are in the power of the tongue" (Proverbs 18:21), and I used mine to kill everything around me, including the plants in Mom's flowerpots. She blamed it on her lack of a green thumb, but she had never had an issue growing petunias until I sat by them spewing poison. The more I provoked this kind of negativity, the less I could stand to hear myself talk. I realized my toxic attitude misrepresented the mentally tough, loving girl who still existed deep within me, the girl who desperately desired to leave the injured reserve list and re-enter the game.

• • •

At least once every basketball season, I rolled my ankle. It swelled until I couldn't see the bone, leaving me hobbling for weeks. Refusing to miss out on playing time, I embarked on a regimen of anti-inflammatories, pain-relieving gels, elevation, and icing, until the flesh deflated and turned from black to purple, green, yellow, and back to normal. The athletic trainer taped me up, I Velcroed on a brace, and back to the court I'd go. I even taped my ankles and wore braces when I wasn't hurt—just in case.

Senior year, I entered physical therapy after my most painful sprain. Rehabilitation began in a whirlpool, where I regained range of motion by rotating my foot to spell the alphabet. As I progressed, I balanced on a single leg to build stability and performed different squats to restore my strength. I also improved my core and leg muscles to build a stronger foundation and reduce future injuries. None of the exercises felt good, but the process promoted recovery, which I tried to speed up.

After three weeks, I wanted to play so badly I jogged around convincing my coaches and myself I was good to go. I returned to the court only to end up back on the bench with a swollen ankle before the game ever started. I couldn't simply slap on some tape, lace my shoes tightly, and will myself healthy. Because I denied my ligaments adequate time to heal, I only reversed my progress and damaged my mindset as I watched others play.

I tried to repair my relational injuries in a similar way. After I wrote off a person who hurt me, I disengaged socially and waited for the bruises to disappear. Bandaging my ego with a few prayers,

I rushed back into relationships, forcing friendships, further hurting myself and dragging others along with me.

• • •

Emma and I met through an anti-bullying organization. She was the first person I really connected with about bullying, and I thought that made us an instant match. Over two years we developed a friendship; we emailed mostly, talked on the phone, occasionally met for lunch, and celebrated a Fourth of July together. She was kind, but over time, I realized how little we had in common. I laughed about things Emma didn't think were funny. She'd stare at me straight-faced then change the subject to a more serious topic, which, even though we were the same age, made me feel like I was talking with a stuffy old lady. On the inside I'd stick my tongue out at her, but on the outside, I acted like it didn't bother me. I thought if I laughed more, she'd eventually loosen up. Even my family said we didn't seem compatible, but I pushed aside all doubts because Emma came into my life when I needed someone. I had to either deal with our differences or I wouldn't have a friend.

Have you ever gotten yourself into something you wish you hadn't? When Emma asked me to be a bridesmaid, I jumped at the opportunity without asking what the responsibility entailed, and Emma only told me as we went along. In the following months, as she planned her big day, Emma flipped from respectful to demanding. She'd call to ask my opinion, only to reject my ideas. "No, I don't like that," she'd say. Or, "Um, yeah, I don't think so." There wasn't anything wrong with saying no. It was how she said no that bugged me, using a sixth-grade Sara kind of tone. *If you don't want my ideas, why ask?* I thought. But instead of saying what I felt, I grew more intolerant of her every phone call.

I cringed listening to Emma talk about her plans. She was inviting hundreds of guests and wearing a puffy princess dress with a tiara. I didn't want to talk about tiaras. They made me think of high school. Neither did I want to spend hours talking about white versus cream-colored linens or paper versus cloth napkins. I had just started my career, and I had stuff to do. You'd think I would've learned from my experience with Hayley, but I didn't connect the two. I just wanted Emma to make her own decisions and let me off the phone.

I hadn't done any of this stuff for my own wedding, a low-key event with only eight family members in attendance. I wore a halter dress that cost less than a hundred dollars. I didn't even want a bouquet until my mom persuaded me. The ten of us hiked to an overlook, speckling ourselves with sweat. Our decoration was the sunset over the red rocks of Sedona, Arizona. Now I understand why those frills were important to Emma. She wanted what she wanted just like I wanted what I wanted. There was nothing wrong with either, but at the time, I found her tastes so unrelatable that I gritted my teeth every time she called to talk. Outwardly I complimented her ideas, but inside I wasn't empathetic.

I reached my limit when she texted me plans about taking two bachelorette trips, one local and one to Vegas, sky diving and eating at ritzy restaurants. All I could think was, *How do I get out of this?* My husband and I were just married and struggling financially. *How does she think I'm gonna pay for all of this?* I thought a friend who really knew me would never require me to do such a thing. Maybe she thought a friend should be willing to do whatever she wanted. Maybe it's standard practice to drop that kind of money on a wedding, or easier when it's a best friend. I should never have agreed to be Emma's bridesmaid without understanding what I was in for, not only for my sake but also hers. I realized we didn't know each other that well, and we weren't the best friends I wished we could be. Not only did I want out of the trips, I wanted out of the wedding.

Do I suck this up or go through with it? I didn't want to hurt Emma, but I hadn't figured out how to tell her what I was thinking. I stalled for two weeks, avoiding her calls and giving her the same kind of I'm-so-busy excuses I hated others giving me. When my HVAC unit went out, I thought it was the sign I had been waiting for. I texted, *Hey, Emma. I just found out we need to replace our HVAC unit. I'm sorry, but I can't afford to go on these trips.*

Looking back, I think of my parents at the kitchen table with their yellow legal pad, and I realize what I meant was I don't *want* to afford to go on these trips. I could've used my savings, asked my parents for a loan, or added the expense to a mounting credit card, but I didn't think it was fair to burden myself or anyone else with something I didn't feel strongly about. I could've asked Emma if it would be okay if I simply stood by her side on the most memorable day of her life, or if I could watch from the pews with the other guests. But I didn't offer another solution, because I just wanted out of the friendship. *It's a six-thousand-dollar unit,* I wrote. *I don't know how we're gonna pay for it.*

I assumed she would understand, but all Emma texted was, *I'm really disappointed.*

I hated those words. No matter who said them, they thrust me back to high school faster than any others. Emma probably meant she was disappointed I didn't want to go on the trips, but all I heard her say was, "I'm disappointed in you, you failure. You're such a bad friend. No wonder you don't have friends." Now I realize what I heard were my own words.

The screw-you attitude I tried to contain inside my family's pool fence infiltrated my phone. I couldn't speak all that negativity into existence and not expect to see it take shape in my life. *I don't think I should be in your wedding*, I wrote. *Hopefully this is enough time for you to find a replacement.*

That was the last time we talked.

Emma tried calling a few weeks later, but I never answered. My no-reply was most uncharacteristic. When I had issues with my college roommates, I wanted them to talk to me so we could work out our problems. Now I had someone willing to pick up the phone, but I refused to cooperate. I should've returned Emma's call. When I think of the texts that have left me hurt, it's not as much the text itself but everything the text left unanswered. I now know that if I'm going to deliver hard news, I should have the courtesy to pick up the phone. It's what I would want someone to do for me. That way there are less whys and what-did-I-dos. Emma deserved to tell me how she felt and to know how I felt, and I wish I could've told her gracefully, but it was easier to go silent.

As I reflect on both of us having been bullied, I see how the two of us limped our way through our friendship. Neither of us had other friends, and both of us had expectations neither was meant to fill at that time. We tried to work with what we had, forcing the friendship forward when we should've released each other. Unfortunately, I needed this experience so that I didn't repeat it. I'm just sorry Emma had to be my learning tool.

• • •

I treated friendship like I treated my sprained ankles. I wanted it so badly that I rushed back into relationships like I rushed back into games. I never prayed about it. I only listened to my emotions, focusing on what I needed others to be to me and not what I could be to them. As a result, I ended up benched with self-inflicted injuries of the heart. If I was going to find my way back to friendship, I needed to rehabilitate in a way I never had before. I had to go deeper to fix the core problem, like I did with my physical therapist when I built a stronger foundation that would help me reduce future injuries. So, I returned to the only Therapist who could help me solve every problem.

Jesus not only knew the pain of being bullied, He knew the pain of having been bullied. He knew the void left by friends. The depression that followed. Lies that materialized. And the expectation of repeated hurt. Although He devotedly served people, few were concerned for His well-being, for getting to know Him as intimately as He desired to know them. Often depleted, Jesus withdrew to lonely places to seek solitude, intimacy with the Father, direction, and restoration.

When I felt beaten down, Jesus showed me I could step away periodically, not to sulk, not to control how people treated me, but to let people be people and to revive my compassion by bringing my issues to God. I couldn't stay in isolation because Jesus never stayed in isolation. He continually returned to people because to love people is to commune with them. Jesus never gave up on others, not even when they hurt Him in the worst possible ways. Because people mattered that much to Jesus, they needed to matter that much to me. My being bullied, my fumbling through friendships, did not justify my calloused heart. I couldn't let my love grow cold because others' love grew cold. (Matthew 24:12, 13) But how could I love others when I so often didn't even like others?

"Show me," I said to God, who taught me that true healing begins by taking ownership of my attitude and making every thought obedient to Christ. (2 Corinthians 10:5) Where God favored me, Satan, the biggest bully of all time, targeted my most valuable attributes. Through my friendliness, he frustrated me with unfriendliness. He used rejection to upset me and disloyalty to offend me. By realizing the enemy's scheme to play on my past and hijack my thinking, I gained the upper hand. With God, I could defy the lies.

God didn't create eight billion people for me to throw my hands up over a few failures. Jesus warned me I wouldn't get along with everyone. I'd experience conflicts and ongoing rejection, but that didn't give me an excuse to renounce people. God created me to share my gifts with others. He wants me to experience the rewards of friendship and community. So I started looking for the "goodness of the Lord in the land of the living." (Psalms 27:13)

As I sought confirmation of God's promises, my views shifted. When people fired me up, I asked questions to expand my perspective rather than assign blame. "God, why would that person do that?" "Why do I feel this way?" and "How can I see her differently?" The more I asked, and the longer I sat still in those questions, the more God cultivated a heart of love within me.

MY FIRST HOME

POOLSIDE AT MY
CHILDHOOD HOME

DAD, MOM, MATTIE, AND ME POSING
FOR THE CHURCH DIRECTORY

DAD COMMENDING US AS
BIDDY BALL CHAMPIONS

ESCORTED ACROSS THE FIELD AS
FRESHMAN HOMECOMING ATTENDANT

SUPPORTING MY FRIENDS ON
THE FOOTBALL TEAM

AT THE STATE TOURNAMENT
MY JUNIOR YEAR

WILLING MYSELF TO SMILE DURING THE
HOMECOMING PEP RALLY MY SENIOR YEAR

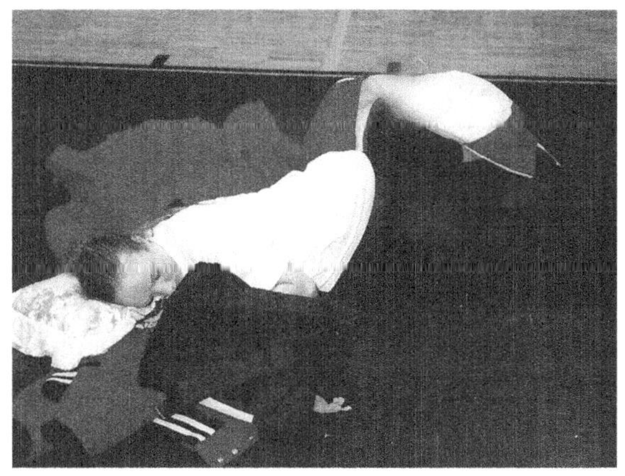

EXHAUSTED AFTER A BASKETBALL GAME MY SENIOR YEAR

COLLEGE GRADUATION WITH MY BOYFRIEND, CHARLIE, WHO I LATER MARRIED

• • •

After high school, I saw Chelsea more than any Bee. Every time, she snapped at the sight of me, once jawing me out of a retail store I had just entered. As I distanced myself from confrontation, I started seeing Chelsea from afar. One day, from the safety of my car, I watched her walk across a grocery store parking lot when I was reminded of the words of Jesus: "Father, forgive them, for they do not know what they are doing." (Luke 23:34) For once, I felt no need to defend myself or escape. Through my windshield, Chelsea appeared differently than ever before. She was no longer my opponent but a reflection of my mistakes and limitations. In her, I saw myself loved by God when I acted unlovable. For the first time, I truly regretted hurting Tyler. For rushing into arguments with the Bees. For telling Kevin to never come back. For slamming Liz and Katie's door and not looking up more from my books to talk to Hayley. For writing off people when I felt wronged. For categorizing everyone associated with my hurt as bullies. And for saying people sucked. Through Chelsea, I saw my classmates and myself as vulnerable young people simply trying to navigate our inadequacies, figure out our identities, and belong. And I wanted better for all of us. The more I improved my thinking and extended the same grace to others that I asked for myself, the less I saw the reflection of my bullies in people and the more I desired re-engagement.

I couldn't just pray for relationships and watch them fall into my lap, though. I had to enter environments that disrupted my distorted views. I searched for a church, attended conferences, listened to an acquaintance's business proposal, and met clients for lunch. I reached out to a former friend, talked to strangers at the grocery store, learned peoples' names, and extended compliments. I even attended parties when I preferred to stay home with my cat. I decided I'd bring my best to every situation, extending what I wished to attract. The least I could do was brighten someone's day. It's what I had been good at, and I needed to tap back into that power.

At first it was uncomfortable. When I smiled my jaw tightened. Words emerged awkwardly. But the more often I acted the more natural it became, until I enjoyed sharing me regardless of what others thought or I gained. My efforts didn't work every time. Some people ignored me or stared at me with furrowed brows and gaping mouths. More people accepted me with gladness. When I focused on what I could bring to others, I released the pressure to replace what I had lost. I could love others, not to regain their affection but to glorify God, from whom all relationships flowed. Because I remained obedient in this step for years, I healed relationally. I couldn't heal alone, though. I had to let others help me, whether they knew that's what they were doing or not.

• • •

My husband, Charlie, and I own a fitness business. When we were first married, we struggled to stay in operation. Something had to change, so Charlie joined a local business group called FitStar, organized by successful entrepreneurs in our industry. I expected Charlie to receive mentorship on how to improve our business. Other than that, I didn't think there was anything in it for me. Charlie spent months trying to get me to go with him, but I pushed it off as his thing, not mine. Every time he returned home, he relayed his friends' desire to meet me. Feeling pressured to do something I wasn't sure I wanted to do, I resisted. "Why do they want to meet me?" I snapped.

"Because I talk about you, and you're an important part of our business."

"Eh, they're probably just saying that to make you think they care," I said.

This wasn't like chitchatting with the mailman. I couldn't believe that anyone wanted to meet me without me initiating the interaction. It was what I had wanted for so long, and when it happened, it scared me. After months of Charlie's persuasion, I could no longer contain my curiosity about these people, so I agreed to go.

From the moment I received my first handshake from Coach E, an esteemed former NCAA Division 1 strength and conditioning coach, I knew I'd return. He was more excited to meet me than anyone I had met since college, but also chill about it. "Tami! Charlie tells me you're the heart of the business," he said. I immediately felt important. "Have you met Natalie?" he asked. Natalie organized the meetings. She and her husband, Chris, were former gym owners and knew the challenges of running a fitness business. By implementing ideas from the group, they were able to sell their gym and venture into other areas of the health and wellness industry. Charlie and I wanted to expand into other areas as well, so we gravitated toward them and listened to their advice. From here, we would rely on Coach E, Chris, and Natalie as some of our closest mentors.

Charlie, Coach E, Natalie, and Chris introduced me to others. "You remind me of so-and-so," they'd say. "Let me introduce you." They connected me with people who shared my interests, desired to know me better, and embraced my personality. They kept me so busy meeting people, and everyone was so nice that I didn't even think about looking for negative signals or what could go wrong. The group wasn't only about business but valued personal growth. Many of the members were also Christians. People were vulnerable. They shared their screw-ups, what they wanted out of life, and their refusal to allow others' opinions to diminish their impact. They were cut-the-fluff kind of people—my kind of people—and their convictions made me want to keep coming back.

For two years I tested these relationships, thinking that if I stayed around long enough, they'd eventually push me aside. Instead, they greeted new people just like they welcomed me without making me feel less valued. And it motivated me to do the same for others. Getting hurt became a distant afterthought. I enjoyed the game so much that I stopped playing taped up and braced for rejection. Through each positive encounter, I found myself smiling more, starting conversations, laughing louder, and staying longer.

I felt myself becoming more like the me I was before I was bullied. I opened up and made friends who invited me to events, mailed me hand-written cards, and gifted me books. We traveled and shared meals together, and our families got to know one another, sort of like the camaraderie I experienced in youth on my AAU basketball teams. When I anticipated gossip and one-upping, I discovered people who celebrated each other's growth, which encouraged inclusiveness. We used our strengths to compensate for others' weaknesses, even when it meant receiving nothing in return. If someone struggled to help a client, another would call or meet the client with us, simply to provide third-party encouragement. Our clients couldn't believe we made the effort to find them additional support without additional costs. Helping one another was just what we did because it was the right thing to do. And when problems arose amongst our group, we tackled them directly, asking questions to gain understanding.

The world wanted me to doubt that this kind of people existed, to believe that they were too good to be true, but that was a lie. With an improved mind, I allowed them into my heart without begging for acknowledgment. I could belong again when I surrendered my need for belonging to God.

My FitStar friends not only helped transform our business, they brought me back to that place that Mom and Dad had established, where relationships were the heart of life and made everything better. And it confirmed what I had learned from Jesus—that people need people. Because I had a place and a people again, I returned to the loving girl God created me to be.

After ten years, FitStar dissolved. The leaders of the group went different directions in life. Dynamics changed amongst the remaining members, and the group lost its drive to gather, causing most of us to go our separate ways. I didn't want to lose what we had there, but when I felt myself forcing some of those friendships on, I remembered Emma, and I let go, finding peace in the release.

Charlie still talks to Coach E, Natalie and I text once in a while, and I'm always uplifted to send and receive Christmas cards from other friends. Our time together reminds me that most friendships have a season. Just because that season ends doesn't mean I need to categorize it as a loss. My FitStar friends were some of the best relationships of my adult life. They proved to me that, even when it feels uncomfortable, meeting new people and taking the time to wait on the right people is worth the effort. Through them, God gave me back what I had lost and more, deepening my heart for others and my hope in friendships to come.

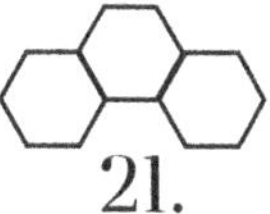

21.
THE IMPRINT OF BULLYING

AS A TEENAGER, I dreamed of taking a wrecking ball to my high school. Ten years ago, taxpayers did the job for me. Since I graduated, most of my administrators and teachers had retired, and, per state law, the school had adopted an anti-bullying policy. I returned once to see my sister graduate. The Honeybees no longer bother me. Sara married her high school sweetheart. Their children, like most Honeybee children, attend our alma mater.

Two years after I saw Chelsea walk across the grocery store parking lot, I ran into her again. She calmly requested my attention and initiated our apologies. Because God loved and forgave me, I could love and forgive her, not only through a windshield but up close. After I learned Chelsea had become a Christian, I realized she had understood this too. It was this experience that taught me I could view my bullies not as who they were but as who Chelsea proved they could become. Our faith provided the reason for us to message on social media about Janeen's passing. And why I know that if we ever see each other again, we will greet one another kindly.

As forcefully as I've tried to erase high school, it stays with me. Just when I pack it away, it's unboxed all over again through random memories, a song, a dream, or perhaps more than anything, social media. The homecoming queen sent me a friend request, and I still don't know why. A year later, I saw her in a restaurant. I half smiled. She passed without speaking. It's been five years since I accepted her request, and we've never communicated. I occasionally see her posts, like the rant she shared after her child's classmates targeted his achievements. I saw his picture once. Dressed in our school's colors, he gripped a football just like his dad, who had been the captain of the football team. It makes me wonder if they regret acting like the kids whose behaviors they now condemn, or if they deny the correlation.

The same classmate who tagged me in a photo from homecoming tagged me again in a photo of a newspaper clipping captioned "Three seniors vie for the crown." What is sweet nostalgia for some and an opportunity to react with laughing emojis for others is an occasion to which I'd rather not return, but in a flash, I'm back in those hallways. As I stare at the picture, processing the memory, I see words I can't unsee. A friend of Tyler's comments that he doesn't know who I am. I know who he is, though. I never forgot. I scroll over his name, revealing his cover photo of a football player leaning over a fallen opponent. "Bullying . . . it comes with a price," the picture reads. His comment buzzes like a honeybee searching for nectar. The pain of feeling forgotten is unforgettable, but I don't have to live in it. I don't even have to spend five minutes in it. Once again, I remove the tag and turn off the notifications.

As many times as I close social media windows, the imprint of bullying remains. It's not so much the names they called me or the rumors they spread, but the defining moments that changed my relationships forever: when I discovered that human beings are selfish, that I could fall prey to them, and that I am one of them.

The world tells bullied kids to leave our narrow-minded small towns; but gossips, joy stealers, and dream killers aren't exclusive to Main Street, nor are their tactics restricted to teenage girls. We are encouraged to seek revenge through impressive job titles and by showing off our filtered families and homes to thousands of social media followers who will dote on images to envy. But this extended popularity contest is a game I won't play. No amount of trophies or admiration rectifies the wrongs done against me or protects me from mistreatment.

I used to think bullying had ruined me, but there are worse things than becoming an outcast. I won't curse my hometown. I won't reprimand people for what they kept and I lost. Some people may hold my mistakes over me forever, but I no longer punish myself for what God has forgiven or for what fostered my growth. While I'm sorry for my retaliation, I wouldn't change anything to soften the pain that profoundly impacted me. What I gained is too valuable to suppress, so I share it to help others who see their stories reflected in mine.

It's easy to remember the bad stuff. I'd rather direct my mind to precious memories: four seniors hand-in-hand during a locker room prayer; my favorite teacher, who mails me a Christmas card every year; the classmate who wrote me an encouraging note I keep in a shoebox; the sound of Annie's laughter; the girls of the Red Rover chain; my biddy ball teammates; and the one friend I think about more than anyone.

On a crisp afternoon, walking a path at Mom and Dad's, a gleam of white catches my attention. It's one of Kevin's golf balls, lodged into a bank. As I thumb off the dirt, the whoosh of our bike race brushes the side of my face. The wafting smoke of a bonfire reminds me of how we met. Hugged by the rolling hills of the woods we grew up in, I forget about the what-went-wrongs. For a moment, I glide into untainted friendship, where I'm innocent and invincible, secure and significant.

I wish I could tell you that I never think about the friends I lost, but sometimes my heart hurts for who they were and who I know they'll never be again. Allowing myself to reflect on the treasures of friendship doesn't deny the bullying, nor does remembering the bullying diminish the beauty of it all. For the totality of my experience led me to my most cherished prize, a prize I could never earn, refuse to relinquish, and no one can ever take away.

Never again will I surrender my value to the opinions of others. No one can make me feel less-than when I am deemed more-than. No name defines me. No rumor disgraces me. I'm not who they say I am. I am who God says I am. My worth is in Jesus, who suffered at the hands of bullies on my behalf to reveal His unconditional love for me. In Him, I'm crowned royalty, dressed in my dad's intensity, my mom's patience, and every strength and flaw that makes me, me. I smile unapologetically. Under pressure, I call upon my tough-mindedness. Struggle strengthens me. I'm kind, direct, and unashamed of my fighting spirit. I won't weaken my gifts to accommodate others' insecurities or compromise my identity to gain their approval. I walk in the lasting confidence of the Lord. The more I embrace His definition of success, the less

I'm defined by this world and the better I'm able to give grace to those who come against me.

Gossip, bad-mouthing, backstabbing, and betrayal can create a swarm, but I'll only get stung if I start swinging. I can't always control how others treat me, but I can decide how to react. I don't need to combat cutthroats or highlight others' wrongs to protect myself. I let the bees buzz. They'll fly away.

Over the years, as friends enter and exit, I've often felt like a failure. Sometimes I'm so eager to secure a connection that I talk too much, only to be met with silence. I've forced friendships that were never meant to evolve to fill the void left by former pals, and I've attempted to resurrect relationships that should stay in the past. Sometimes I expect way more from people than they can give and project the past onto others when I should treat them without bias. I try to remember that friendship isn't supposed to be like it was; it's supposed to be like it is. The more aware I become of the effects of bullying on my interactions, the less my baggage holds me back from trying again.

My struggle to regain deep connections reminds me that I belong to God's kingdom, where I don't need to earn my way in or compete for His love. Because I know this, I can love people. I can allow relationships to go where they'll go. If they don't go anywhere, I accept it as a sign that I'll discover compatibility elsewhere. Trustworthy people exist. I might have to search diligently to find them or put myself out there when I'd rather stay hidden, but they are worth the effort. I can form solid relationships by remaining open and focusing on what I can give over what I can get.

I understand I'm not a match for everyone, nor are they for me. Conflict is inevitable, but not all conflict constitutes bullying.

I can work through problems to preserve the connections I value, careful not to take people for granted. I strive to learn something from everyone, giving them room to grow just as I want for myself.

When I'm offended, I don't need to rush into an argument like it's a checkmark on my to-do list. I don't need to unload a piece of my mind every time something doesn't go my way. Before addressing a problem, I seek the whole story from its source and, in prayer, reflect upon my emotions. If God guides me into confrontation, I can express myself gently and firmly, relaying what I think because I think before I speak. I can collaborate with others without compromising my integrity. Each new conflict teaches me more about when and how to raise my voice and when to step away. Because even when I know the entire story, sometimes it's better to keep the peace than fight to prove my point. Sometimes it takes more guts to stand still than to stand up. Standing still doesn't necessarily mean doing nothing. It means surrendering to God because I trust who He is. The best way to raise my fist is to let Him fight my battles.

No matter how thoughtfully I conduct myself in a relationship, I'm not guaranteed to solve every problem or keep the connection. Sometimes it's best to release it. Disagreements don't need to end badly, but if they do, I can exit with compassion, even for those who choose not to act kindly in return. I don't have to live in loss every time relationships change. I can establish boundaries without writing people off. I can use disappointment as a signal to grow my love and move forward in relationships without attaching the pains of my past.

In this world, when you stand for anything, you become a target. Whenever you exceed expectations and disrupt dynamics, prepare to upset someone. Some people won't like you because they want for themselves the strength they see in you. Some people create drama because they're bored. Others participate in that drama because they're trying to figure out how to communicate. Still, some people believe the only way they can win is at the expense of your well-being. Through covert methods, they criticize, twist the truth, harass you to your limit, and cause chaos in your relationships, all while waiting to capitalize on your missteps.

When you are the target of unchecked envy. When words become weapons from people you never expected to hurt you. When your reputation is blemished, friends betray you, or you lose the only community you've ever known. When you feel unwanted and alone, and the enemy whispers lies built on the pain of your past, remember the words of Jesus: "If the world hates you, keep in mind that it hated me first. If you belonged to the world, it would love you as its own. As it is, you do not belong to the world, but I have chosen you out of the world. That is why the world hates you." (John 15:18,19)

People don't determine your value. Don't grant them that power. You aren't who they say you are. You are who God says you are, fearfully and wonderfully created to honor and serve Him. (Psalms 139:14)

The burdens inflicted on you at your most vulnerable, impressionable moments are no longer yours to carry. Hand them over to Jesus, who understands your hurt like no one else ever could. He absorbed all the unkindness the world will ever bring against you so you could know His unconditional love, your undeniable worth, and healing. Standing on His unshakable foundation frees you from the shame bullies may have brought on you. Jesus is the Friend who will never leave and who helps you forgive when you can't seem to forget. If He is for you, who can be against you? (Romans 8:31)

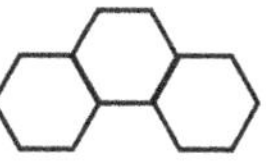

ACKNOWLEDGMENTS

THANK YOU to everyone who has followed my story through the years, given me the grace to grow, and patiently awaited the completion of this project. Every inquiry provided me confirmation that my story was worth sharing.

It has been amazing to see Holy Spirit move through this process and connect me to one person after another.

Thank you to my Charlie, who watched me sit at our kitchen table and peck at my computer day after day. Thank you for listening and helping me articulate my thoughts when I got stuck. When I felt guilty for not producing much, you always assured me my hard work would pay off, and my words would impact others.

Thank you to my most loyal supporters, my parents. Mom, through your ability to write eloquently, and Dad, through your gift of storytelling, both of you inspired my creativity.

Thank you to Mattie, for your spirited encouragement and for asking me, "How's it going" at the precise moment I doubted it was going.

Shawna Green, thank you for critiquing my first page. You

gave me the courage to move to the next step.

Heather Shaw, it's wild that God sent me an editor who specialized in memoir before I knew I needed one. Your gift of seeing the whole picture helped me develop and complete my story, and I'm grateful to you.

And to Emily and Clair of the Columbus Publishing Lab, thank you for embracing my ideas, supporting my decisions, and guiding me through the publication process. Your expertise was vital to the smooth production of this book.

NOTES

1. Merten, Don E. "The Meaning of Meanness: Popularity, Competition, and Conflict Among Junior High School Girls." *Sociology of Education* 70 (1997): 181. "During sixth grade, attractiveness to boys became increasingly important."

2. Simmons, Rachel. *Odd Girl Out: The Hidden Culture of Aggression in Girls.* New York: Harcourt, 2002: 46, 80. "Silence throws up an impenetrable wall, shutting down the chance for self-expression and, more importantly, the opportunity to play a proactive role in one's conflicts," and rallying peers' support "provides a way for girls to displace their aggression while remaining connected to others."

3. Ibid p.16. "Girls target you where they know you're weakest."

4. Ibid p. 75. "For these girls, absorbing anger is just as frightful as voicing it. The idea that they may be 'at fault' or 'wrong' makes them uneasy, and it can breed panic and impulsive decision-making. In many cases, they grasp for whatever will move the harsh spotlight away from them and onto someone else. Raised in a culture that prizes sweetness, what feels right to these girls is an

anxious scramble to remain the 'good' girl; to hold up a mirror to their friend and, instead of listening, point out a past infraction. Needless to say, such conflicts escalate swiftly, often leaving both girls filled with regret and fear."

5. Ibid p.79-84. "Nothing launches a girl faster, or takes her down harder, than alliance building, or 'ganging up.' The ultimate relational aggression, alliance building forces the victim to face not only the potential loss of the relationship with her opponent, but with many of her friends. It goes like this: Spotting a conflict on the horizon, a girl will begin a scrupulous underground campaign to best her opponent. Like a skilled politician, she will methodically build a coalition of other girls willing to throw their support behind her. Friends who have 'endorsed' her will ignore the target, lobby others for support, or confront the target directly until she is partly or completely isolated. Ganging up is the product of a secret relational ecosystem that flourishes in an atmosphere where direct conflict between individuals is forbidden. By engaging in conflict as a group, no one girl is ever directly responsible for her aggression. Anger is often conveyed wordlessly, and the façade of the group functions as an eave under which a girl can preserve her 'nice girl' image. Alliance building also conforms to girls' tendency to stockpile old conflicts. The perpetrator's strategy is to appeal to those who have a history with the target. Particularly where girls have known each other for many years, the perpetrator can plumb a rich history of relational trouble."

6. Adler, Patricia and Adler, Peter. "Dynamics of Inclusion and Exclusion in Preadolescent Cliques," *Social Psychology Quarterly* 58 (1995): 154. "Other classmates tended to side with the dominate

people over the subordinates, not only because they admired their prestige but also because they respected and feared the power of the strong. They knew that clique members banded together versus outsiders, and that they themselves could easily become the next target of attack if they challenged them."

7. Merten, Don E. "The Meaning of Meanness: Popularity, Competition, and Conflict Among Junior High School Girls." *Sociology of Education* 70 (1997): 184. "As the popularity of one girl increases, the popularity of another decreases."

8. Garbarino, James and Ellen deLara. *And Words Can Hurt Forever: How to Protect Adolescents from Bullying, Harassment, and Emotional Violence.* New York: The Free Press, 2002, p.15, 84, 120. "Approximately one-third of the students admitted that they had approached an adult in the [school] building with what they considered to be a serious concern, but they were not 'listened to' or 'taken seriously,' and that 'nothing had changed as a result of their attempts.' School systems are extremely slow to change, and because of this there is a 'critical breakdown in any attempt to build a systematic solution to enhance safety and reduce violence.'"

9. Simmons, Rachel. *Odd Girl Out: The Hidden Culture of Aggression in Girls.* New York: Harcourt, 2002, p.201. "That girls who engage in direct conflict may have little real social power is a sad irony, to say the least. The assertiveness shown by some minority girls may reflect not self-confidence but their vulnerability in larger society. In many instances forthrightness stems from the girls' senses that they can only make themselves heard by using physical force or dangerous speech."

10. Merten, Don E. "The Meaning of Meanness: Popularity, Competition, and Conflict Among Junior High School Girls." *Sociology of Education* 70 (1997): 176, 187-189. "Girls were discouraged from acknowledging their competition even when competition for popularity was pervasive." A girl who enjoyed popularity was "most vulnerable to being labeled stuck-up." It was "a common cultural dilemma to seek popularity, but when they were successful, to pretend they were not popular. Popular girls enhanced their chances for continued popularity by being nice. Popularity was as problematic as it was desired. When something highly valued cannot be openly expressed, alternative forms of expression are often invoked. We do not know how to justify status obligations and hierarchical relationships, but we live them."

11. Siobhan S. Pattwell, Francis S. Lee, and B.J. Casey. "Fear learning and memory across adolescent development." *Hormones and Behavior Special Issue: Puberty and Adolescence* 64, Issue 2 (2013): 380-389.

12. Garbarino, James and Ellen deLara. *And Words Can Hurt Forever: How to Protect Adolescents from Bullying, Harassment, and Emotional Violence.* New York: The Free Press, 2002, p.123. "Scapegoats are often the people in the system who are most sensitive to what is going on. Systems utilize scapegoats as a means to resist change; if there is someone to blame, then no one has to look to himself or herself for personal change to make things better. Some children are scapegoated or stigmatized based on physical attributes, specific mannerisms, or ways they behave. Others are scapegoated because of some special experience or history they have, like being the new kid in a school or having done something

embarrassing that becomes part of the peer folklore.

"Children learn from us, and they too engage in scapegoating others. Children tend to blame the kids who are targeted by bullies for the bad treatment they receive. They see the victims as weak, nerds, or as deserving what they get.

"At school, kids who are bullied are thus scapegoated by the system many times over— first by the bullies, and a second time by the other kids who see them as causing their own problems. The process continues when the system (in this instance, the school's adults) does not step in and intervene in an effective way on their behalf. Of course, kids are directly scapegoated within the system when they are bullied or intimidated by teachers, coaches, and other school personnel who ridicule or tease for their own reasons. The poisonous process comes full circle when adult participation in scapegoating ensures that the other children will see these kids as 'fair game.' However confusing or complex this dance may appear to you, you need to believe that you are witnessing a strong warning sign of an ailing system. This is not the kind of system that can or will support the healthy growth of children."

13. Campbell, Anne. *Men, Women, and Aggression: From Rage in Marriage to Violence in the Streets—How Gender Affects the Way We Act.* New York: Basic Books, 1993, p. 18, 50, 56. "When a woman does reach the limit of her self-control and strikes out, men tend to be dumbstruck. Her behavior does not fit the representation of coercion and power through which they view it and thus seems unpredictable and pointless. Women's aggression, unlike men's, is not directly aimed at establishing physical victory. Women explode as a means of release. For her, physical aggression

is about losing, not winning. Women's anger often erupts from being manipulated or humiliated by their superiors."

14. Simmons, Rachel. *Odd Girl Out: The Hidden Culture of Aggression in Girls.* New York: Harcourt, 2002, p.82. "Alliance building is a sign of peer affirmation, an unspoken contract that means, for the moment anyway, that a girl will not be abandoned." Adler, Patricia and Adler, Peter, "Dynamics of Inclusion and Exclusion in Preadolescent Cliques," Social Psychology Quarterly 58 (1995): 151, 153-154. "In friendship realignment, clique members abandoned previous friendships or destroyed existing ones in order to assert themselves as part of relationships with those in central positions. Turning people against an outsider solidified the group and asserted the power of the strong over the vulnerability of the weak."

ABOUT THE AUTHOR

AS A WRITER, speaker, and businesswoman for the past 20 years, Tami has shared her story with thousands. She is also a fitness coach who has inspired thousands to healthier lifestyles. She and her husband, Charlie, live in Ohio with their kitties.

Download Tami's free guide, *Seven Steps to Healing After You're Bullied*, and follow her stories about faith, fitness, friendship, and felines at tamimccandlish.com.

Made in United States
Orlando, FL
07 March 2023

30795037R00136